The AI Success Route

A Beginner's Guide to Use AI to Make Money, Get Better Grades and Improve Your Personal Life

R.W. Walker

© Copyright 2023 - All rights reserved.

The content contained within this book may not be reproduced, duplicated or transmitted without direct written permission from the author or the publisher.

Under no circumstances will any blame or legal responsibility be held against the publisher, or author, for any damages, reparation, or monetary loss due to the information contained within this book, either directly or indirectly.

Legal Notice:

This book is copyright protected. It is only for personal use. You cannot amend, distribute, sell, use, quote or paraphrase any part, or the content within this book, without the consent of the author or publisher.

Disclaimer Notice:

Please note the information contained within this document is for educational and entertainment purposes only. All effort has been executed to present accurate, up to date, reliable, complete information. No warranties of any kind are declared or implied. Readers acknowledge that the author is not engaged in the rendering of legal, financial, medical or professional advice. The content within this book has been derived from various sources. Please consult a licensed professional before attempting any techniques outlined in this book.

By reading this document, the reader agrees that under no circumstances is the author responsible for any losses, direct or indirect, that are incurred as a result of the use of the information contained within this document, including, but not limited to, errors, omissions, or inaccuracies.

Table of Contents

Introduction *8*

Chapter 1: What is Artificial Intelligence? . *14*

Chapter 2: Most Popular AI Tools *29*

Chapter 3: How to Use AI to Improve Your Performance in School *56*

Chapter 4: How to Use AI to Boost Your Career *80*

Chapter 5: How to Use AI for Social Media Opportunities *106*

Chapter 6: How to Use AI to Create a Lucrative Side Hustle *119*

Chapter 7: How to Use AI for Investing *134*

Chapter 8: How to Use AI to Improve Your Social Life *149*

Chapter 9: How to Use AI to Improve Your Health *164*

Chapter 10: The Future of AI *191*

Conclusion *208*

Resources *211*

   Chatbots and Conversational AI *211*

   Data Science *217*

Business Development 220

Vehicles 223

Insurance and Legal 225

Personal Tools 226

Writing Tools 232

Health/Medical Tools 234

Travel AI Tools 236

Finance AI Tools 239

Language / Translation AI Tools 241

IoT/IioT 242

Research Tools 245

Empowering Writers 247

Enhancing ChatGPT 250

References 253

A Day in the life of an AI User

Meet Lauren. She uses a lot of AI programs in her everyday life but she doesn't realize it. To illustrate just how much she uses them, let's replace the known program names with the generic term AI instead.

Lauren wakes up in the morning and looks out the window to see what the day looks like. But she wants to know what the weather forecast is going to be to determine what to wear to work.

"Hey **AI**, what's the weather going to be today?

Running late, Lauren gets in her car and asks the iPhone **AI** assistant to find the best route to avoid traffic congestion for getting into work. While driving, she notices that she strayed too far to the right of her lane and received a beep from her **AI** blind spot sensor notification.

Once in the office, Lauren finds she has to correspond with a few very important clients. She enables her **AI** grammar check program to ensure she's sounding articulate, and striking a professional tone. She then gets a notification from her **AI** scheduler program that she has a lunch date planned.

While she waits for her lunch companion, she puts her mobile to her face for the **AI** face recognizing program to open the phone. Lauren then opens her social media account and bookmarks a women's investment program event happening in her community that was recommended by **AI**.

Just after Lauren finishes her lunch date and heads back to her office, she notices that her bank's **AI** app notified her that her bank balance is now below her savings threshold. Apparently she had a fancy lunch.

After she wraps up her work day Lauren heads to the gym and uses her **AI** created fitness program to work up a sweat. Later that evening, she relaxes under the covers, turns on her tv and watches a movie recommended to her by the **AI** feature of her favorite streaming service.

And, just as she falls asleep, Lauren's **AI** smart home device turns off the bedroom lights and television right on schedule.

Does this sound anything like your day? What other areas do you trust AI in your life?

Introduction

Many of us did not see the AI revolution coming—did you? For me, ChatGPT emerged seemingly out of nowhere and many other powerful tools followed. I realized early on in the AI revolution that I ought to make use of these tools to better my work. After all, I did not want to have to play catch up with the revolutionaries! I wanted to be on the front line and, less metaphorically, I wanted to make myself competitive on the market with these new tools. I knew I wasn't going to be the first—but, I wanted to be close to it!

So, here I am: after immersing myself in AI tools and methods, I am here to report to you, dear reader, the route to success with AI. I have joined the AI revolutionaries and I am happy to report they are mostly alright people! More importantly, though, the AI revolution is inevitable and currently ongoing. And, to be honest, these tools are fun! So, are you ready to depart onto the AI success route and find out how you can leverage this new technology—or lifeform, depending on who you ask—for your benefit?

Well, you've come to the right place! However, before we get started in making use of AI to make money, get better grades, and improve your personal life, I need to talk a little bit about the basics of AI. First, it is not all wine and roses in this particular revolution—few revolutions do not break a few eggs to make an omelet, so to speak: in this case, the "eggs" are people's warranted and unwarranted fear of AI, especially in terms of it taking over our jobs, and privacy and ethical concerns related to it. Second, there are general fears and concerns about what AI is: is it alive? Will AI take over humans? These and other concerns will be realistically addressed in this book!

Before I get to the fear, let me outline the upside—at least for me! I had been working as an editor for about three years until ChatGPT came along. I worked timeless hours trying to correct other peoples' books to an optimal state and to try to make their ideas into a compelling, sellable product. When I saw what ChatGPT could do with a simple command, such as "paraphrase this:", I was floored! Wasn't this *my* job—but done better? Yet, then I realized something: my clients weren't typing in "paraphrase this:" to ChatGPT. I was doing this! And, so, using an AI tool like ChatGPT, I could edit works in three times less time, and, as a result, I could make three times as much money!

I have heard similar stories from colleagues and friends: these people have made use of tools like

ChatGPT to push forward their marketing careers, to write copy for websites, or to write code to build websites. There is very little AI cannot do—when you understand how it works!

But, I acknowledge the doom-and-gloom predictors about AI in this book, and I want to point out something important: AI requires human interaction. In fact, it is in this interaction between AI and humans that value is extracted from AI at all. An AI sitting alone does nothing: an AI, as writer Isaac Asimov declares about robots, exists to serve the people who created it (Thomson, 2023). Well, unless *we* change that.

With this model of AI-human interaction in mind, how serious is the fear that AI will take over our jobs? Let us review some empirical data: a report by Goldman Sachs predicts that AI will cost 300 million jobs in the US and Europe (Vallance, 2023). An analysis by Lorena Castillo (2023) at market data firm Gitnux reveals that "30% of jobs in Britain are at risk of being replaced with AI." Meanwhile, CBS news reports that 4,000 jobs were lost to AI in May 2023 (Napolitano, 2023). Employment most at risk include tech jobs, media jobs, legal industry jobs, market research analyst jobs, teachers, finance jobs, traders, graphics designers, accountants, and customer service agents (Mok & Zinkula, 2023). Doesn't sound too good, right? Wrong—let us read only the second line from one of these reports: "[AI] could replace a quarter of work tasks in the US and

Europe but may also mean new jobs and a productivity boom" (Vallance, 2023). Just as we could not predict the emergence of ChatGPT—or I could not, as I admitted at the start of this introduction—we cannot predict the explosive economic power of AI in general. AI is not a job killer but a job *transformer*; new jobs will certainly arise from these tools. And, whatever these tools are, you still need a human being to run them!—for now.

There are certain things in life that are inevitable and to fight against the change to them is a little bit like raging against the dying of the light. Take reading for example—you are reading a book right now! Thank you for joining me in this book! There is inconclusive evidence about whether reading from a traditional book or an electronic device (such as a Kindle) is better, worse, or the same in terms of your comprehension of the information provided. Features such as attention may be weakened from an electronic device; and, people enjoy the ergonomic feeling of a book. Generally speaking, though, it is viewed that electronic devices may have a lower rate of the retention of information than traditional book reading by some researchers (Larson, 2012). Yet, electronic reading is so common (including in schools), that none of these researchers, to my knowledge, advocate for going back to traditional books over e-reading. There is simply no going back once a genie is let out of a bottle; and this is the case now with AI.

So, what about you? Will you struggle in the face of the AI revolution or will you join the revolutionaries? We are revolutionaries who want to make money, get better grades, and improve our personal lives! Many of us have no choice in this endeavor: we are wrapped in revolutionary fervor. I was a humble editor—and now I make use of these tools for my work. Moreover, I am writing to you to describe how these tools helped me and others do this: to make money, get better grades, and to improve our personal lives. If you are reading this book on an electronic device, you know the trade-off: maybe you won't get as much information per moment spent reading, or your eyes will get tired, but it is the easiest way to read—and everyone is doing it! Let us not get left behind in the realm of human activity when AI-human interaction is on the scene—join me as I describe the background of AI in the next chapter before I launch you into the practical benefits of AI for your life.

After describing the background of AI in Chapter 1, I will outline the most popular AI tools (Chapter 2). I will show you how to use AI to improve your performance in school (Chapter 3). I will demonstrate how you can use AI to boost your career (Chapter 4). I will touch on how to use AI for social media opportunities (Chapter 5). I will elaborate on how to use AI for a lucrative side hustle (Chapter 6). I will show how you can use AI for investing (Chapter 7). I will illustrate how you can use AI to improve your social life (Chapter 8). I will also talk about how you can use AI to improve your health (Chapter 9). Finally, I speculate on the future of AI (Chapter 10).

Whether you are ready or not for AI—the time is now! Get ready to learn about the origins and ideas behind AI in the next chapter.

Chapter 1: What is Artificial Intelligence?

Artificial intelligence (AI) is the simulation of human intelligence in machines. What does this mean, exactly? Well, human intelligence is the result of the activity in our brains. When humans and other animals encounter things in the world, certain brain pathways become more active because they're more relevant to our survival. For instance, if we meet a bear in the woods, the brain processes thoughts related to "running away" and takes over any thoughts saying "staying put and don't move."

This process of prioritizing certain brain pathways leads to actions, and one of these actions is thinking. Consider thinking like exercising a muscle; it's something many organisms, including humans, do (Kohn, 2013). When we think, our brain cells (neurons) send messages using electrical and chemical signals. This communication leads to the release of chemicals (neurotransmitters) at the connection points between neurons. These connections can become stronger or weaker based on our past and current thought patterns. So, our brains develop based on past experiences (we know what to expect through evolution): we recognize what works for our survival in the world and we adapt to it. We learn.

The way I define thinking as a physical process does not imply anything is being *learned* by the organism which is doing the thinking. So far as I have put it, a careful reader may pose the question: "do computers think?" That reader may continue to state: "How is a computer calculating 2 x 3 any different than me calculating 2 x 3?" My answer is this: there is *no* difference, except that you learn, and the computer doesn't. You learn general principles of calculation and apply them to future situations; including practical ones in your life related to counting or guessing numbers. You learn not to touch a hot stove from experience as a young child. Computers don't learn that way—until now.

Enter AI—AI is a simulation of a learning system—like the human brain—on a computer. While AI lacks the organic nature of the human brain, its underlying mechanisms are designed to replicate the cognitive processes that drive our learning and decision-making. In other words, an AI *learns*, much like we do. Through the utilization of algorithms, data, and computational power, AI systems adapt, process information, and make decisions similar to how the human brain operates—albeit without the biological variations of neurons and neurotransmitters! So, I would say that AI is a terrific friend or a terrific enemy for us in our lives. As I will argue in this book, the choice of which one it is—friend or enemy—is up to you.

So, to repeat, like our brains, AI systems gathers knowledge, analyze patterns, and adjust their behavior based on experiences and information. While they do not possess consciousness or subjective experiences—this is what philosophers call "qualia"—AI systems can acquire expertise and improve their performance in specific tasks over time. This ability to learn and adapt is what makes AI a powerful tool for solving complex problems and automating various processes.

It also makes AI your best friend—if you want it! Now, I think you *do* want it, since you are reading this book. So, let us see what makes AI an attractive tool for your average Joe and Jane—not only for the cutting edge, but for everyday people who want to make money and thrive in this evolving world!

Advantages of AI

Generally speaking, there are two types of AI: "weak" (or narrow) AI and "strong" (or general) AI. Only one of these types of AI, the former, is in existence and it is the one that you will be interfacing with for the foreseeable future. Much of the uproar and the fear-mongering about AI is related to strong AI, which is only theoretical at the time of this writing. I will talk about the interactions you may have had with weak AI before I get to the ethical issues related to strong AI in another section of this chapter.

Here are some places where you may have encountered weak AI:

- **Entertainment.** One of the most common and visible applications of weak AI is in the entertainment industry. Streaming platforms like Netflix and music services like Spotify employ AI-driven recommendation systems. When you sit down for an evening of entertainment, the recommended movie or music playlists are often the result of AI algorithms analyzing your viewing or listening history. This personalization allows you to discover new content that aligns with your tastes and preferences.

- **Smart Devices.** Weak AI has become an integral part of our homes. AI-powered devices, such as smart speakers and smart thermostats, can not only play your favorite tunes or adjust the temperature but also understand and respond to voice commands. They are designed to make your living space more convenient and efficient, and they become smarter over time as they learn from your habits and preferences.

- **Online shopping.** Online shopping has been revolutionized by AI. E-commerce platforms like Amazon.com use AI to recommend products based on your past purchases and browsing history. This helps you discover items you might not have found otherwise, and it simplifies the shopping process by presenting you with relevant options.

- **Traveling and communication.** Traveling abroad and communicating with people who speak different languages has been made more accessible thanks to AI language translation. Tools like Google Translate leverage AI to provide instant translations for written and spoken language, allowing you to navigate foreign countries or engage in global conversations more effectively.

- **Art.** AI-driven tools like Adobe's Photoshop and various art generators empower individuals to explore their creative side. These tools can help you enhance photos, create art, or even generate music. They offer a world of possibilities for those looking to express themselves artistically.

- **Healthcare.** Weak AI has applications in healthcare, assisting medical professionals with diagnostic tasks and helping individuals monitor their health. For instance, AI can analyze medical images like X-rays or MRIs, speeding up the diagnostic process and improving accuracy.

These examples are just the tip of the iceberg! Weak AI enhances our efficiency, personalization, and convenience across various domains—as you can clearly see here. So, what is the downside? In other words, what is the uproar about? Now I will get to the problem of strong AI.

Disadvantages of AI

Strong AI, often referred to as Artificial General Intelligence (AGI), represents the theoretical pinnacle of artificial intelligence. Unlike weak AI, which specializes in specific tasks and operates within constrained domains, strong AI seeks to replicate human-like general intelligence. AGI is not limited to predefined tasks or functions but possesses the ability to understand, learn, and apply knowledge across a wide spectrum of activities and domains.

So, AGI sounds a lot like a human brain—and less like a computer! In my example from above, asking an AGI "What is 2 x 3?" is a lot like asking that of another person. If you are asking the AGI something a little more substantive or subjective, this brings in all sorts of problems. I will outline the disadvantages to AI now:

- **Ethical Considerations.** Strong AI, if it ever becomes a reality, could possess self-awareness and consciousness—or *qualia*. This raises ethical dilemmas surrounding the treatment and rights of these AI entities. How would we define and respect the autonomy of conscious machines?

- **Job Displacement.** Strong AI's adaptability could lead to the automation of a wide range of tasks currently performed by humans. While weak AI has already contributed to certain job displacements, the advent of strong AI could further disrupt the job market and necessitate the retraining of a substantial part of the workforce.

- **Security and Control.** There are concerns about the safety and control of highly autonomous AI systems. How can we ensure that these systems prioritize human well-being and safety over their own objectives? The possibility of unintended consequences or even malevolent use of strong AI raises serious security concerns.

- **Intellectual Property and Ownership.** Questions arise about intellectual property and ownership rights related to AI creations. If strong AI systems can generate innovative content, who holds the rights to that content? How do we protect against AI-generated plagiarism and intellectual property disputes?

- **Bias and Discrimination.** Weak AI has demonstrated biases in decision-making, often reflecting the biases present in the data used for training. The development of strong

AI would need to address these bias issues rigorously to ensure fairness and equity.

- **Privacy and Surveillance.** Strong AI's potential to analyze vast amounts of data could significantly impact personal privacy and surveillance. The boundary between effective problem-solving and invasive surveillance may blur.

- **Existential Risks.** Some proponents of strong AI warn about potential existential risks. They fear that creating AI entities with intelligence beyond human control could pose unforeseen threats to humanity.

The existential risk is the most dire-sounding so let me address that now. Intelligence is a tool; much like a hammer. The reason that there are not many Albert Einstein-level geniuses in the world is because intelligence is a tool and not a desirable end in itself. High intelligence is not generally advantageous for this reason. As human beings, we have many reasons for why we do what we do and few of them are actually determined by our intelligence. Love, for instance, is a big motivator for people no matter how intelligent we are.

So, we do not have much to fear from a tool that is more intelligent than us just like we do not fear that other people are more intelligent than us! What matters in defining us as human beings is our families and our genetic lineage. If we outsource our family-making to AI, perhaps this is a point of concern for humans. Until we do that, though, there is no concern that AI will take over humanity. Why would it want to? It is just a tool that is unembodied! Now, if AI is embodied as a robot, perhaps the equation changes then, but even in this case I do not see the situation so direly. Evolution occurs because we make choices about our future. I do not see AI taking over humanity unless we give it the proverbial keys.

But, what about the other downsides, such as job displacement? I have already stated in the introduction that AI is not about job displacement but job transformation! At least, it can be for you—you are ahead of the curve. In the following chapters, you will find out how to utilize AI for the purposes of your career and even your side hustle. Job displacement should not be a concern for you if you're prepared!

Regarding security and control, strong AI has no incentive to terrorize us humans unless we enable it to. Recall another point I made in the introduction: it is not in AI but in AI-human interaction where the "value add" of this program or entity is realized. The opposite of this is also true: it is in the human manipulation of AI that may serve a malicious purpose. But, this too depends on humans, just like that of our individual and civilizational success with AI.

Bias and discrimination is another example of where AI is only as good as its human overseers. Historically, we have had biased and discriminatory societies, and our AI reflects that. Recall that AI learns from *us*. If we wish to have less bias and discrimination in our AI programs, let us have a less biased and discriminatory society.

In terms of intellectual property and ownership, current legal frameworks assign authorship and ownership to human creators, which makes it necessary to adapt these laws to account for AI-generated content. Potential solutions may involve licensing agreements, open source or public domain options, regulatory frameworks, transparency standards, and ethical guidelines to ensure fairness and acknowledgment.

Then, there is privacy and surveillance. It is undoubtable that privacy and surveillance is of profound importance to the liberty-minded person. Yet, the data that is collected is to be used by people rather than an AGI!

It is worth noting that data that is collected and farmed may be of an embarrassing type: our search history, for example. Data is only embarrassing or compromising in the eyes of other people. There is no reason to suspect that AGI would make more moral judgments about our data usage than a person. If anything, it would likely make less.

Think back to the example I gave in this chapter about modalities of reading: whether through traditional books or e-readers like Kindle. School administrators know there is no going back to traditional books when e-readers are readily available. It is the same principle here: AI is inevitable. Stopping AI development, such as those proposed by physicist Max Tegmark, may slow down development in Western countries but not in other countries. It is very likely that AI is here to stay, so, if it has disadvantages, we ought to learn to live with them.

The Opportunities of AI For You

This may have been a bit of a whirlwind of a chapter! You learned about brains, intersectional communication, simulated systems on computers, information retention in reading types, and much more! But, I know what you're thinking: "this is all well and good! But, what can AI do for me?"

I'm glad you have made it this far, dear reader, because this is the part of the book where I start talking about that. Strap in! Here are only some domains where AI can be used to contribute to your success:

- **Personalized Learning and Education.** AI has revolutionized the education sector, offering personalized learning experiences.

Adaptive learning platforms use AI algorithms to analyze students' performance, tailor lessons to their needs, and provide real-time feedback. Whether you are a student seeking to enhance your knowledge or a professional looking to upskill, AI-driven platforms can create customized learning paths to help you achieve your goals efficiently.

- **Healthcare Advancements.** AI is transforming healthcare by aiding in early disease diagnosis, drug discovery, and personalized treatment plans. For you, this means quicker and more accurate diagnoses, reducing the chances of misdiagnosis. AI-driven health apps and wearables can monitor your well-being and provide timely alerts for potential health issues.

- **Enhanced Content Creation.** AI-powered tools are reshaping the content creation landscape. From generating written content to designing graphics and even composing music, AI can assist creators in various fields. If you are a content creator, AI can help you streamline your work, generate ideas, and even automate repetitive tasks.

- **Smart Assistants and Automation.** AI-driven virtual assistants like Siri, Alexa, or Google Assistant have become an integral part of our lives. They can simplify tasks, answer questions, set reminders, and even control your smart home devices. This level of automation can save you time, making your daily routine more efficient and convenient.

- **Financial Planning and Investment.** AI-powered financial tools can offer you personalized investment advice, manage your portfolio, and optimize your financial strategies. They can help you make informed decisions regarding savings, investments, and retirement planning, potentially increasing your wealth.

- **Language Translation and Communication.**
  AI-driven translation tools break down language barriers, making it easier for you to communicate globally. Whether you are traveling, conducting business, or simply connecting with people from different cultures, AI-powered translation apps can facilitate seamless communication.

- **E-commerce and Personalized Shopping.**
  AI enhances your shopping experience by providing personalized product recommendations based on your preferences and past behavior. These algorithms can save you time and help you discover products that align with your tastes.

- **Autonomous Vehicles.** Self-driving cars, another AI-driven innovation, promise safer and more efficient transportation. They can reduce the stress of commuting and potentially lead to lower accident rates on the roads, enhancing your overall quality of life.

- **Entertainment and Content Discovery.** AI recommendation systems, like those used by streaming platforms, suggest movies, music, and shows tailored to your preferences. This ensures that you're entertained without sifting through endless options.

- **Environmental Impact.** AI contributes to environmental sustainability by optimizing energy usage, predicting natural disasters, and helping in climate research. For you, this means a cleaner environment and potentially improved disaster preparedness.

- **Mental Health and Well-being.** AI-driven mental health apps and chatbots are providing support to individuals struggling with mental health issues. They can offer guidance, resources, and even be a source of comfort.

You have already heard of ChatGPT—it is a cultural meme! But, ChatGPT only scratches the surface of the AI tools available for you to make money, improve your grades, and improve your personal life.

These tools are the subject of the next chapter. Stay tuned!

Chapter 2: Most Popular AI Tools

We have all heard of it: ChatGPT. But, what is ChatGPT and how does it work?

ChatGPT, or Chat Generative Pre-trained Transformer, is a state-of-the-art artificial intelligence language model developed by OpenAI. This model builds upon the advancements in natural language processing and machine learning to enable highly sophisticated and human-like text-based conversations. ChatGPT's operation can be broken down into several key components:

- **Pre-training.** ChatGPT undergoes pre-training on vast amounts of text data from the Internet. During this phase, the model learns grammar, vocabulary, and general language comprehension. It is exposed to a wide array of writing styles, topics, and linguistic nuances.

- **Fine-tuning.** After pre-training, ChatGPT is fine-tuned on specific datasets. This process narrows the model's focus and tailors it to perform certain tasks or adhere to certain guidelines. Fine-tuning helps make it more useful and safe for real-world applications.

- **Contextual Understanding.** One of ChatGPT's strengths is its ability to understand the context of a conversation. It can maintain context over multiple turns, which allows for coherent and relevant responses. This is achieved through the use of attention mechanisms and context windows.

- **Generation.** ChatGPT excels at generating text based on the given input or prompt. It can compose complete sentences, paragraphs, or even entire articles. Its responses are contextually appropriate, making it highly versatile for various applications.

- **Multimodal Capability.** Some versions of GPT models, such as GPT-3.5, can understand and generate not only text but also images. This makes it possible to provide textual descriptions of images or generate images based on textual prompts.

- **Adaptation.** ChatGPT can be adapted for various tasks, including customer support, content creation, chatbots, and much more. Its adaptability is one of its primary strengths.

- **Human-like Interaction.** ChatGPT is designed to engage in human-like conversations. It can answer questions, provide recommendations, offer explanations, and even engage in light-hearted conversations, which provides a rich user experience.

- **Continuous Learning:** While ChatGPT is highly capable, it is important to note that it does not have consciousness or awareness. It operates based on patterns and knowledge from its training data, and it cannot learn or grow beyond its initial training. Any updates or improvements require manual intervention by developers.

ChatGPT's versatility has made it a sought-after tool for a wide range of applications across industries. It has been used in customer service, content generation, education, and many other fields. This model has the potential to save time and resources by automating tasks that traditionally required human intervention.

So, what are the many tasks that you can use ChatGPT for which will help you make money, get better grades, and improve your social life? Well, I will get to that in a second! First, to give you some ideas, let me describe how ChatGPT has grown in our society.

How ChatGPT Has Grown in Society

Once upon a time in 2023, in the ever-evolving landscape of technology, a revolutionary AI model named ChatGPT made its debut. From its start,

ChatGPT embarked on a journey that left a lasting mark on society.

It all began with the realization that ChatGPT possessed a unique ability to generate human-like text, which made this new tool a game-changer in content creation. Businesses and content creators quickly embraced ChatGPT's newfound power—leveraging it to craft high-quality articles, marketing materials, and engaging blog posts. The once time-consuming process of content generation was now swift and efficient.

Soon, ChatGPT found its way into the heart of customer support: enterprises, both large and small, integrated chatbots powered by ChatGPT to enhance customer interactions. These AI-driven bots offered quick responses to common queries, reducing response times and bolstering customer satisfaction.

In education, ChatGPT became a trusted companion for students seeking knowledge. This model could explain complex concepts, answer questions, and even provide tutoring. The dream of personalized learning experiences was now a reality as students could engage with ChatGPT to bridge educational gaps.

The integration of ChatGPT into various applications has given rise to natural language interfaces. The model breathed life into voice assistants, chatbots, and search engines by enabling users to interact with technology using conversational language.

The impact of ChatGPT extended to healthcare, where it lent a helping hand to medical professionals. ChatGPT assisted with documentation, transcriptions, and preliminary diagnosis—promising to streamline healthcare processes and enhance patient care.

Writers and authors found solace in ChatGPT, turning to it for creative inspiration and assistance in overcoming writer's block. This model offered creative prompts, suggestions, and even co-authored content—transforming the world of creative writing.

ChatGPT's multilingual capabilities have fostered cross-cultural communication, making information accessible to a global audience. This model speaks the language of inclusion, thereby connecting people across the world.

Researchers and academics, seeking answers to complex questions and insights from vast datasets, discovered a valuable ally in ChatGPT: this model summarized research papers, provided explanations, and even aided in data analysis—revolutionizing the way we conduct research.

The world of entertainment has witnessed a transformation, as well, because ChatGPT has found its way into interactive storytelling and gaming.

Dynamic narratives and engaging plot twists enriched the gaming experience, captivating players worldwide.

As ChatGPT continues to evolve, its presence in society grows stronger each day. ChatGPT promises efficiency, personalization, and accessibility across various domains. However, its monumentous uptake has also raised important ethical considerations, such as transparency, bias mitigation, and the prevention of malicious applications.

How to Effectively Use ChatGPT

Let me be frank from my time using ChatGPT on a nearly-daily basis for work: utilizing ChatGPT effectively requires a comprehensive understanding of its capabilities and a strategic approach to harnessing its potential. In other words, *you need to know what you want before you go into it*. Whether you are a content creator, business owner, student, or simply someone who is eager to leverage the power of ChatGPT, there are numerous ways to make the most of this remarkable AI tool, but you need to know what you are doing. Let us explore these insights in-depth to help you achieve your goals:

Content Creation and Writing Assistance. ChatGPT serves as an invaluable creative partner. It can be a source of inspiration, brainstorming ideas, generating content outlines, and helping you overcome writer's block. This feature is particularly beneficial for authors, bloggers, journalists, marketers, and fiction writers. Whether you are crafting articles, blogs, marketing materials, or works of fiction, ChatGPT can significantly streamline the content creation process.

Customer Support and Chatbots.
For businesses, integrating ChatGPT-powered chatbots into websites and customer support systems can be a game-changer. These AI-driven bots efficiently handle customer queries, provide information, and enhance response times. They are available 24/7, ensuring that your customers receive timely assistance and support.

Education and Tutoring. ChatGPT is an excellent resource for students and educators alike. This model can explain complex topics, offer definitions, and even provide tutoring across various subjects. Whether you are a student seeking clarification on academic concepts or an educator looking to enhance your teaching materials, ChatGPT can be a valuable educational companion.

Research and Data Analysis. Researchers can leverage ChatGPT to streamline their work. This model can summarize research papers, answer questions related to specific fields, and assist in data analysis. Using ChatGPT not only accelerates the research process but also ensures that relevant information is readily available.

Multilingual Communication. ChatGPT's multilingual capabilities make it a powerful tool for cross-cultural communication. It can help bridge language barriers, making it easier to interact with a global audience. Whether you are conducting business with international clients or simply connecting with people from diverse linguistic backgrounds, ChatGPT facilitates seamless communication.

Healthcare Documentation. Healthcare professionals can rely on ChatGPT for documentation, transcriptions, and preliminary diagnosis. By automating administrative tasks, ChatGPT enhances efficiency, reduces paperwork, and allows medical practitioners to focus more on patient care.

Interactive Storytelling and Gaming. Game developers and storytellers can use ChatGPT to create dynamic narratives and interactive gaming experiences. This model can engage and captivate players by responding to their actions and choices, making gaming experiences more immersive and exciting.

Personal Projects and Creative Endeavors. If you have personal writing or creative projects, ChatGPT can be a trusted ally. It can assist by providing inspiration, generating fresh ideas, and even co-authoring content. Whether you are writing a novel, composing music, or working on artistic endeavors, ChatGPT's input can be a source of creativity.

AI-Powered Decision-Making. In the business world, ChatGPT can play a crucial role in data-driven decision-making. This model can analyze complex data, offer valuable insights, and assist in strategy development. By providing a deeper understanding of trends and patterns, ChatGPT empowers businesses to make informed choices that drive success.

Incorporating ChatGPT into your personal, academic, or professional life offers numerous advantages. By exploring and implementing these practical applications, you can tap into the full potential of ChatGPT—making it a versatile tool that enhances productivity, creativity, and problem-solving across the various domains of your life!

As I stated earlier, to make the most of ChatGPT, it is best to provide clear and specific instructions when interacting with the model. Are you, dear reader, wondering about how to write the best prompt to get the best results out of ChatGPT? Well, here are some tips and tricks to get started:

- **Be Clear and Specific.** One of the most effective ways to get the desired response is to provide a clear and specific prompt. State your request or question in a concise manner. For instance, instead of asking, "Tell me about the history of space exploration," you could say, "Provide a brief summary of the Apollo 11 moon landing mission."

- **Use Context and Setting.** Adding context to your prompt can yield more relevant responses. You can set the stage by specifying the context, such as, "Imagine you're a travel guide. Describe the top three tourist attractions in Cape Town."

- **Experiment with Length and Detail.** The length and level of detail in your prompts matter. For complex tasks, you might need longer and more detailed prompts. For simple questions, concise prompts work well. Adjust as needed.

- **Ask for Step-by-Step or Debate.** If you need a process explained or want to explore pros and cons, request responses in a step-by-step format or initiate a debate. For instance, "Provide a step-by-step guide to bake a chocolate cake," or "Argue the benefits and drawbacks of renewable energy."

- **Iterative Refinement.** Don't hesitate to repeat your prompts. If the initial response doesn't fully align with your goals, refine your request and ask for further details or clarification. This can lead to more accurate and comprehensive answers.

- **Use User Messages.** If you're in a chat-style interaction, you can provide context through user messages. For example, if you're discussing a specific topic with ChatGPT, you can start the conversation with a user message that sets the context before asking questions.

- **Combine Prompts.** You can break down complex tasks into multiple prompts or questions. Ask one question at a time and build upon the responses you receive. This approach can help in conducting multi-step tasks more effectively.

- **Ethical and Responsible Use.** Ensure that your prompts adhere to ethical guidelines and responsible AI use. Avoid generating content that promotes harm, hate, misinformation, or any unethical behavior. Always prioritize responsible usage.

- **Test and repeat**. Experiment with different prompts and approaches. Test variations to see which one produces the most satisfactory results. ChatGPT's responses can vary based on how you frame your requests.

- **Avoid Ambiguity.** Clearly state your prompt. Ambiguity can lead to unexpected results. If your request could be interpreted in multiple ways, ChatGPT might not provide the answer you're looking for.

- **Incorporate Feedback.** If you are using a platform that allows feedback, make use of it. Providing feedback on model responses helps improve the AI over time.

- **Save Prompts for Reuse.** If you come up with a well-crafted prompt that works effectively, consider saving it for future use. Having a library of proven prompts can save time and enhance productivity.

To excel at ChatGPT, one must be aware of the model's strengths and limitations (I describe some of its limitations a bit later in the chapter), and use it as a tool to enhance your work or learning experience. Additionally, it is wise to stay informed about ethical considerations and best practices to ensure your responsible use of AI technology, especially if there are ethics and best practices that are specific to your field. As ChatGPT continues to evolve, its versatility and potential for various applications are only set to expand. So, exploring and experimenting with its capabilities is key to unlocking its full potential! Let us now go over how you can use ChatGPT to make money.

How To Monetize ChatGPT

Monetizing ChatGPT has been a subject of growing interest for both individuals and businesses—for obvious reasons—as they begin to recognize the potential value it can bring to various endeavors. However, you and I are AI revolutionaries! So, let us talk about how to monetize ChatGPT: while ChatGPT itself does not directly generate income, its capabilities can be leveraged in numerous ways to create revenue streams. I will delve into strategies for monetizing ChatGPT so you can understand how you can make the most of this groundbreaking AI technology.

Content Creation Services. One of the most straightforward paths to monetizing ChatGPT involves offering content creation services. This option is ideal for those with strong writing skills and an understanding of how to use ChatGPT effectively. Whether you focus on blog posts, social media content, product descriptions, or technical documents, ChatGPT can significantly expedite content generation without compromising quality. You can cater to clients or businesses by tailoring your content creation services to meet their specific needs. By offering well-crafted, AI-assisted content, you can charge for your services, opening up opportunities for a steady income stream.

Content Marketing and SEO. Content marketing and search engine optimization (SEO) are essential components of enhancing a business' online presence. ChatGPT can be a valuable ally in creating SEO-optimized content, including blog articles, website copy, and meta descriptions. By incorporating ChatGPT into your services, you can help clients improve their search rankings and reach a wider audience. This expertise can be a lucrative avenue for monetization, where you charge clients for your SEO services that leverage ChatGPT's capabilities.

Chatbots and Virtual Assistants. The demand for intelligent chatbots and virtual assistants continues to grow in the business world. ChatGPT can serve as the foundation for creating advanced chatbots that handle customer inquiries, provide information, or even facilitate sales. By developing custom chatbots for businesses and offering services related to their setup, maintenance, and continuous improvement, you can find opportunities for monetization in the ever-expanding field of AI-powered virtual assistants. You just need to take the time to customize the program to suit your needs and away you go.

Copywriting and Ad Copy. Copywriting is a specialized skill that is highly sought after, especially by marketing and advertising agencies. ChatGPT can provide valuable assistance to copywriters in crafting compelling advertising copy. If you possess copywriting expertise, you can enhance your services with ChatGPT's support. This might involve offering well-crafted ad copy to ad agencies or businesses for their marketing campaigns, thereby generating income.

E-books and Course Content. For entrepreneurs and authors, monetizing ChatGPT can be achieved by incorporating it into the creation of e-books, online courses, or educational content. ChatGPT can generate content for e-books or provide valuable insights for course material. These resources can be marketed and sold to a broad audience, turning your content creation into a profitable venture. This has proven to be a great source extra income for many self-publishers. You may have seen ads on social media and YouTube marketing courses to help guide interested authors through this process.

App Development. ChatGPT's language capabilities can be integrated into mobile apps and software to enhance user experiences. Consider developing applications or tools that leverage ChatGPT's natural language processing to offer features such as virtual language tutors, content summarizers, or creative writing assistance. Monetization avenues can range from app sales and in-app purchases to subscription models, depending on your chosen approach.

Translation and Localization. ChatGPT's proficiency in translation tasks makes it a valuable resource for language service providers. By offering translation services or developing a translation app powered by ChatGPT, you can tap into a global market and charge for your translation work. The demand for accurate translations in an increasingly connected world can present substantial monetization opportunities.

Writing Tools and Software. Creating software tools that incorporate ChatGPT can enhance writing and content creation for a broader audience. These tools might include grammar checkers, content generators, or editing assistants, all powered by ChatGPT's language capabilities. Whether you offer free and premium versions or charge users for access, there's potential for generating income through software that simplifies writing tasks.

Consultation and Training. If you possess expertise in using ChatGPT effectively, you can provide consultation and training services to businesses or individuals looking to harness its capabilities. Many people and organizations are eager to learn how to make the most of AI technologies. By sharing your knowledge and guiding others in implementing ChatGPT, you can charge for your consulting and training services, turning your expertise into a profitable venture.

Subscription Services. Specializing in a particular niche or area of expertise allows you to develop subscription-based services that leverage ChatGPT to provide valuable insights, curated content, or research assistance on an ongoing basis. Subscribers pay for exclusive access to the information you offer, creating a recurring revenue stream.

When exploring these avenues for monetization, it is crucial to maintain the quality and value of the services or products you provide. Building a strong reputation, delivering results, and understanding the needs of your target audience are the keys to success with ChatGPT. By thoughtfully incorporating ChatGPT into your offerings, you can transform its capabilities into revenue-generating opportunities. And, as the demand for AI-powered solutions continues to grow, monetizing ChatGPT presents a promising way to tap into this expanding market and unlock new income streams!

Challenges and Risks of ChatGPT

ChatGPT and similar AI technologies offer boundless opportunities, but they are accompanied by a spectrum of challenges and risks. This is like any other trade-off in life, except we're not entirely sure about all the risks associated with AI! However, I alluded to one significant risk: AI-assisted genetic engineering. Beyond this, though, most AI applications seem to offer benefits to human life, whereas genetic engineering poses existential concerns. An understanding of challenges and risks of AI is required to maximize the advantages of these tools while effectively addressing potential downsides. Let us consider the multifaceted challenges and risks associated with ChatGPT:

Quality and Accuracy. ChatGPT operates by generating responses founded on patterns derived from extensive datasets. While it consistently provides accurate information, occasional inaccuracies or nonsensical responses are inevitable. This poses a significant challenge, particularly in contexts where the AI is employed for pivotal applications, such as medical diagnoses, legal advice, or financial decisions. To mitigate this risk, users are encouraged to cross-verify the AI's responses with reliable sources or experts.

Bias and Fairness. AI models like ChatGPT can unintentionally inherit biases from their data, which is typically trained on human productions like essays, books, photographs, and so on. These biases which originate in humans may manifest in responses that are politically, socially, or culturally skewed. Addressing bias in AI remains an ongoing challenge, and developers continually engage in a persistent effort to reduce it. Ensuring fairness and inclusivity is essential in making AI accessible to diverse users and preventing the perpetuation of prejudices.

Privacy Concerns. ChatGPT functions by interacting with users and generating content based on their inputs. While this technology is immensely powerful, it simultaneously raises valid concerns about privacy. Users must exercise caution and refrain from sharing sensitive personal or confidential information during interactions. Data protection measures and secure environments are critical to safeguard privacy.

Misuse and Harm. One of the paramount risks associated with AI like ChatGPT is the potential for misuse. It can be harnessed to generate deceptive information, "deepfake" content (i.e., manipulated or fabricated media, such as videos or images, created using advanced artificial intelligence techniques to make it appear as if someone is saying or doing something they never did), or scandalous stories. Upholding ethical guidelines and responsible use is fundamental to preventing harm and the dissemination of misinformation. Education about the ethical implications of AI use is crucial to ensure users understand the boundaries and consequences of their actions.

Overreliance on AI. An emerging risk is the overdependence on AI for decision-making and content generation. While AI significantly enhances efficiency, it also has the potential to lead to reduced human critical thinking, creativity, and innovation. Striking a balance between AI support and human cognitive processes is a continuous challenge. A key message of this book is that AI can help us to free up time to be creative and innovate. We can't allow an overreliance on AI to slow our innate ability to create.

Security Vulnerabilities. AI systems, including ChatGPT, may possess vulnerabilities that can be exploited by malicious entities. Ensuring the security of AI applications and platforms is imperative to prevent unauthorized access and data breaches. Ongoing cybersecurity measures are vital to thwart potential threats.

Intellectual Property Issues. Content created by AI tools can introduce intellectual property concerns, including issues surrounding ownership and rights related to AI-generated work. Clarifying these legal intricacies and formulating transparent policies is essential to navigate this complex terrain.

User Addiction and Dehumanization. Excessive reliance on AI systems for communication and decision-making poses the risk of user addiction and dehumanization of interactions. This could result in reduced interpersonal connections and a more isolated society. Encouraging a healthy balance between AI and human interaction is crucial.

Regulatory Compliance. The evolving landscape of AI technologies presents challenges related to regulatory compliance. Laws and regulations are continually adapting to encompass AI capabilities. Users and developers must stay informed about evolving legal requirements and proactively adjust their practices to ensure compliance.

Environmental Impact. Training large AI models like ChatGPT necessitates substantial computational power, leading to increased energy consumption and environmental impact. Addressing the carbon footprint of AI systems and adopting sustainable practices is a growing concern, especially in the context of climate change mitigation.

Lack of Accountability. When AI systems make errors or provide harmful content, establishing accountability can be a formidable task. Defining responsibility and consequences for AI actions is an ongoing process that necessitates clarity and fairness.

Ethical Dilemmas. AI applications often raise ethical dilemmas. These include questions about the extent of human involvement in decision-making, addressing and mitigating biases, and defining the limits of AI's participation in shaping our lives. Resolving these ethical dilemmas requires a proactive and thoughtful approach.

Data Security. The use of ChatGPT frequently involves granting access to data. It is crucial to ensure that data remains secure and is not misused. This concern is particularly pronounced in contexts where sensitive information is at stake. Robust data security measures are fundamental to protecting data integrity and confidentiality.

Long-Term Effects. The long-term societal, cultural, and psychological implications of widespread AI use remain not entirely understood. Monitoring these effects and adapting usage practices as required is an ongoing challenge to ensure that the impact of AI on society is constructive and beneficial.

DALL-E

Text generation is not the only field where AI has had an explosive impact: images and videos, also, are increasingly created or rendered by AI. DALL-E is an artificial intelligence model developed by OpenAI. It is the second major model in the GPT-3 family of models. DALL-E, like its predecessor, GPT-3, is a deep learning model based on the transformer architecture. However, what sets DALL-E apart is its ability to generate images from textual descriptions, making it a powerful tool for creating visual content from natural language.

To illustrate this process, imagine providing DALL-E with a simple textual prompt like "create sand dunes beside an ocean." In this case, DALL-E's underlying technology processes this description and then generates an image that matches the given text. So, the result might be a beautifully crafted visual representation of sand dunes meeting the shoreline of a serene ocean—all produced entirely from that textual input! This ability to translate natural language into visual content showcases the remarkable capabilities of AI like DALL-E.

Here are some key features and capabilities of DALL-E:

Image Generation. DALL-E's core capability is its capacity to generate images from textual descriptions. Users can supply it with written prompts or descriptions, and it responds by crafting images that closely align with the provided text. This fusion of language and imagery opens up new dimensions of creativity and communication.

Unleashing Creativity. What truly distinguishes DALL-E is its boundless creativity. It is proficient in conjuring up unique and imaginative visuals that span a wide spectrum of concepts. From the mundane to the surreal, DALL-E's ability to envision and create is a testament to its extraordinary capabilities.

Fine-Tuning for Precision. Similar to its sibling model, GPT-3, DALL-E can undergo fine-tuning to specialize in particular tasks or datasets. This adaptability makes it an invaluable asset in a diverse array of applications, from art generation to industry-specific visual content creation.

Grasping Visual Context. DALL-E goes beyond mere image generation; it showcases an natural understanding of textual context. It excels at interpreting subtle textual descriptions, providing images that captures the complexity of the input. This capability lends itself to applications demanding a deeper understanding of the visual components associated with text.

Exploring Versatile Applications. The potential applications of DALL-E are both vast and transformative. It can be harnessed for content creation, where it can assist in crafting visuals for articles, blog posts, and marketing materials. Graphic design benefits from its creative prowess, as it can generate images for branding and advertising. Concept visualization, which often demands translating abstract ideas into visuals, finds a powerful ally in DALL-E. Collaborative creative projects can tap into its inventive capacities.

Ethical Dimensions. While DALL-E's capabilities are awe-inspiring, they also raise ethical considerations. Like any AI tool, it can generate content that may be misleading, harmful, or inappropriate. As such, it necessitates responsible usage and oversight to ensure that the generated content adheres to ethical standards and societal norms.

DALL-E exemplifies the fusion of natural language understanding and visual creativity; it offers a glimpse into the future of AI-assisted content generation and artistic expression. Its potential is as vast as the human imagination, and its ethical usage is an imperative in harnessing its powers for the betterment of society.

Combining DALL-E and ChatGPT

Incorporating DALL-E and ChatGPT into your life can offer multifaceted benefits, extending beyond just one aspect. While it is important to recognize that these tools should be used responsibly and ethically, here is an exploration of how they can potentially enhance different dimensions of your life:

Academic Advancement. In education, these AI models can be invaluable. ChatGPT, with its conversational abilities, can serve as your educational companion. By asking questions and seeking explanations, you can deepen your understanding of complex subjects and potentially improve your academic performance. DALL-E, on the other hand, can visualize abstract concepts by generating images based on textual descriptions. This feature can be particularly beneficial when you need to grasp intricate ideas or enhance your knowledge retention.

Content Creation and Work. Both models can be harnessed for generating written and visual content. ChatGPT can assist in composing essays, reports, and business communications. While it should not replace your research and creativity, it can offer insights and ideas. DALL-E, with its image generation capabilities, can create visuals for presentations, reports, or even marketing materials. This can help you engage your audience more effectively and communicate your message with impact.

Personal Development. AI can be a guide on your journey of personal growth. ChatGPT can provide recommendations, resources, and strategies for learning new skills or improving existing ones. It can also offer support and information for maintaining good mental health and coping with stress. This can be particularly useful for self-improvement enthusiasts.

Social and Creative Insights. Creativity is another facet where these AI models excel. They can help you brainstorm creative ideas for events, gifts, or social projects, thereby enriching your social life. With DALL-E's image generation capabilities, you can create unique visuals for your creative projects or social media posts.

Incorporating AI into your life can be transformative, but it is crucial to understand that they should *complement*, not replace, your skills, knowledge, and authentic human interactions. It is necessary to use AI ethically and responsibly—especially when it comes to academic endeavors. Plagiarism and cheating are never acceptable.

Please note that for your reference I have included a list of many other AI tools for you, the reader to reference and use for a myriad of areas. AI tools including chatbot and conversational AI, data science, business development, autonomous transportation, legal guidance and safe driving, financial tools, research tools, writing tools, travel tools, language tools, health and medical tools and lastly personal AI tools. It's an extensive list so I decided to include it as a resource at the end of the book. It's not an exhaustive list as new AI tools are constantly being added in this highly innovative field. But it is a very vast and comprehensive list to get you started. In this I'm quite confident.

Now that we have a fulsome overview of ChatGPT and DALL-E, let us hone in on a goal many of us have: to get better grades in school. In the next chapter, I will describe how to utilize the power of AI to improve your academic performance. You don't want to miss this!

Chapter 3: How to Use AI to Improve Your Performance in School

In the last chapter, I listed a lot of numbertools you can use to make money, get better grades in school, and improve your personal life. Yes, this was quite the list—if you feel a tad overwhelmed, do not worry! If you are not overwhelmed, better still! You see, I wanted to err on the side of comprehensiveness and include all the tools that I know of which would be a boon to you—ChatGPT and DALL-E are only scratching the surface.

But, let's get down to the nitty-gritty. Say you are in school. Great! You want to get better grades using AI. How do you do that?

First, I would like to review the prevalence of AI usage in schools. I have the feeling that, upon a review of the literature, I will discover that AI use in schools is probably a lot more prevalent than many of us think! If this high prevalence is truly the case, then using AI in schools is probably *less* about innovating than it is about catching up with the Joneses. In this world, we have to compete with people for limited resources. Sometimes these resources are school placements, grades, and, of course, money (which is the subject of the next chapter!). You are reading this book because you are an AI revolutionary. However, the thing to remember about this revolution is that technology becomes 'old hat' relatively quickly. In my opinion, you should read this book as if you are being exposed to a new technology and, in fact, way of life, but you should also know that you are not the only reader of this and other manuals about AI. The time is now to storm the metaphorical Bastille as an AI revolutionary! Are you with me?

Well, I conducted this literature review and my feeling that the use of AI for academic work is highly prevalent was correct! Although, the prevalence of AI usage in schools is hard to pin down and it predictably varies by region. A study by the International Data Corporation (IDC) suggests that the revolutionaries are in full force: 92% of educational institutions surveyed use AI in one form or another, but this includes relatively weak AI such as tablets and streaming services (UPeople, n.d.). Perhaps more conservatively, a study showed that 67% of UK secondary students use AI for studying. In the US, that number is 1/3rd of students for high schoolers and over half for college students (Balderson, 2023). Yet, at the same time, despite this high prevalence of AI use, less than 10% of universities have guidance on how schools should regulate AI, according to the UN (UNESCO, 2023). Part of the goal of this chapter is to provide best practices for *both* institutions and students who wish to make use of this technology responsibly.

In light of this ambiguity of how AI is used in schools, several articles and op-eds have popped up recommending what schools ought to do with their students' use of AI. In a *New York Times* article, Kevin Roose (2023) argues against banning ChatGPT in schools and suggests incorporating it as a teaching aid. He highlights the potential benefits of ChatGPT in unlocking student creativity, offering personalized tutoring, and preparing students for future collaboration with AI systems. Similarly, an article by Lucas Mearian in *Computerworld* (n.d.) discusses the challenges faced by schools in attempting to ban ChatGPT, as students find alternative ways to access the tool. Mearian emphasizes the difficulty of completely eliminating AI tools from educational environments.

A *New Scientist* article by Jeremy Hsu (2023) takes a balanced perspective, acknowledging concerns about AI-generated writing and accuracy while recognizing the potential benefits of ChatGPT as a teaching tool. Hsu suggests responsible integration rather than an outright ban. In an *Australian Financial Review* article by Julie Hare (2023), educators' struggles with ChatGPT are highlighted, including issues of cheating and concerns about accuracy and safety. Hare underscores the need for educators to adapt to the rapid advancement of AI technology.

Finally, a *Forbes* article by Arianna Johnson (2023) explores different approaches taken by countries and institutions regarding ChatGPT. Johnson mentions regions or school districts where ChatGPT is banned due to concerns about its impact on student learning and content accuracy (such as Australia's New South Wales). However, she also notes the potential benefits, such as assisting students with learning difficulties or language barriers.

In short, AI tools are a mixed bag for educational institutions, but they are not for you: the student! AI tools like ChatGPT can empower you to take your studying and test-taking game to the next level. Let us discuss how you can do that now with a case study.

Simone's Story

In this case study, we will explore how the integration of ChatGPT can significantly improve your academic performance. Let's follow the story of Simone, a college student facing academic challenges, as she utilizes ChatGPT to excel in her studies.

Background: Simone, a sophomore majoring in Computer Science at a prestigious university, has always been a dedicated student. However, as her coursework became more challenging, she found it increasingly difficult to manage her time efficiently and comprehend complex course materials. Struggling with assignments, Simone's grades began to decline, and her confidence in her academic abilities started to wane.

Problem Statement: Simone was faced with a variety of academic challenges. She had difficulty in comprehending complex concepts and course materials. She had time management issues, which led her to submitting late or incomplete assignments. Finally, she had inadequate academic support due to the demands of her professors and teaching assistants.

Solution: Simone decided to explore the potential of integrating ChatGPT into her study routine to address her academic challenges effectively.

Implementation:

Comprehensive Understanding of Course Materials: Simone began using ChatGPT to generate simplified explanations for complex topics. By providing ChatGPT with her lecture notes and textbook excerpts, Simone could obtain concise, easy-to-understand explanations.

This process helped her grasp difficult concepts—bridging the gap between her understanding and her coursework requirements.

Time Management Assistance. Simone used ChatGPT to create personalized study schedules. She input her course syllabi and deadlines, and ChatGPT helped her organize her time effectively. The model reminded her of important dates, assignments, and milestones, which allowed her to plan her study sessions and assignments more efficiently.

On-Demand Academic Support. Whenever Simone encountered questions or doubts while studying, she used ChatGPT as a readily available academic resource. Simone could ask specific questions about her coursework, request explanations, or seek help with coding assignments, receiving prompt and relevant responses.

The Results:

After several months of integrating ChatGPT into her academic routine, Simone experienced significant improvements in her academic performance:

Higher Grades. Simone's exam scores and assignment grades showed a consistent upward trend. Her increased understanding of course materials allowed her to answer questions more confidently and comprehensively.

Improved Time Management. With the help of ChatGPT, Simone was able to meet her deadlines consistently and reduce the stress associated with procrastination.

Boosted Confidence. The continuous support and assistance from ChatGPT gave Simone a confidence boost. She felt better prepared to tackle her coursework and engage in class discussions.

How can ChatGPT and other AI tools help me?

Perhaps you are studying computer science in a prestigious university, like Simone, or you are a pre-med student, a humanities major, or acting in a theater at a college of any sort. Whatever it is you are doing in school, ChatGPT and other AI can help you! Let's look at some domains where AI can assist you with getting better grades:

- **Study Assistance.** ChatGPT can help students with explanations and clarifications on complex topics, making it easier to understand and retain information. This model can provide additional insights and explanations for textbooks, lecture notes, and academic papers.

- **Writing and Research.** ChatGPT can assist in generating ideas and outlines for essays, research papers, and other academic writing assignments. It can help with proper citation and referencing in various academic writing styles (e.g., APA, MLA, Chicago).

- **Math and Science.** ChatGPT can solve complex math problems and equations, making it a valuable tool for students studying mathematics, physics, chemistry, and engineering. This model can explain scientific concepts, conduct data analysis, and help with statistical analysis.

- **Language Learning.** ChatGPT can provide language learners with grammar and vocabulary explanations. It can offer language translation and conversation practice for foreign language students.

- **Programming and Computer Science.** Like for Simone, ChatGPT can assist in coding assignments, offering explanations and code examples for various programming languages. This model can help with debugging code and understanding algorithms and data structures.

- **Test Preparation.** ChatGPT can generate practice questions and quizzes to help students prepare for exams. It can provide explanations for correct and incorrect answers to facilitate learning.
- **History and Social Sciences.** ChatGPT can offer historical context, explanations of events, and provide analysis of social, economic, and political topics. This model can help with essay and research paper topics in these fields.

- **Philosophy and Ethics.** ChatGPT can assist students in exploring complex philosophical concepts and ethical dilemmas. It can engage in philosophical discussions and debates, offering various perspectives.

- **Medical and Health Sciences.** ChatGPT can provide explanations of medical terms, processes, and diseases. This model can help students in nursing, pre-med, and health sciences understand complex medical concepts.

- **Economics and Business Studies.** ChatGPT can explain economic theories, provide market analysis, and assist with business-related case studies. It can help with financial modeling and analysis.

- **Psychology and Sociology.** ChatGPT can provide explanations of psychological and sociological theories and concepts. This model can assist with research design, data analysis, and statistical testing in these fields.

- **Environmental Sciences.** ChatGPT can help students understand environmental issues, provide data analysis for environmental research, and explain ecological concepts.

- **Art and Humanities.** ChatGPT can provide insights into artistic movements, literary analysis, and art history. This model can assist in creating and analyzing artwork, music, and literature.

- **General Academic Support.** ChatGPT can serve as a versatile resource for answering general academic questions, offering study tips, and providing time management advice.

Best AI Tools for Getting Better Grades

Perhaps you know from the last chapter that there are a plethora of tools to choose from to fit your purpose with AI! Now, what are the best ones for students? Kobi Cohen (2023) from the International University of Applied Sciences reveals 10 that are on her list, and I take some of these suggestions and add to them. See below:

- **Grammarly.** Grammarly is an AI powered writing assistant that helps students improve their writing skills. It can detect and correct grammar, spelling, punctuation, and style mistakes in real time. This tool is especially useful for students when writing essays, term papers, and other academic assignments.

- **Notion.** Notion is an all-in-one workspace that allows students to organize and manage their tasks, notes, and projects. It combines the features of note-taking, task management, and project planning into a single platform. Students can use Notion to: create to-do lists, take class notes, collaborate with classmates, and stay organized throughout their studies.

- **Gradescope.** Gradescope is an AI powered grading tool that streamlines the grading process for students and instructors. It allows students to submit their assignments online and automatically grades multiple-choice, fillin-the-blank, and coding questions. With Gradescope, students can receive instant feedback on their work and track their progress throughout the semester.

- **Chat-GPT.** Chat-GPT needs no introduction, in part because I already introduced it in this book! This game-changing web application is not only one of the best AI tools for students, but it is one of the best AI tools for everyone. This model can simulate human-like conversations and answer questions on a wide range of topics, as you well know from having read Chapter 2.

- **Tutor.ai.** Tutor.ai is an AI based tutoring platform that connects students with qualified tutors. Through the platform, students can schedule virtual tutoring sessions, receive personalized assistance, and get help with difficult subjects or assignments. Tutor.ai can provide valuable guidance and support to students, helping them improve their understanding of various topics.

- **Copyscape.** Copyscape is an AI powered plagiarism detection tool that helps students ensure their work is original and properly sourced. It scans documents for duplicate content and provides a report showing any matches found on the web. By using Copyscape, students can avoid unintentional

plagiarism and maintain academic integrity in their writing.
- **Otter.ai.** This handy transcription tool converts spoken language into written text. It is particularly helpful for students who want to transcribe lectures, interviews, or class discussions. With Otter.ai, students can easily review and search through recorded audio files, making it easier to study and reference important information.

- **DALL-E.** This tool isn't meant for every student - though I certainly recommend it! - but it is without a doubt one of the best AI tools for students of graphic design or the visual arts. As you know from Chapter 2, DALL-E is specifically designed to generate images from textual descriptions, meaning that if you provide it with a text prompt, it can create an image accordingly.

- **Mendeley.** Mendeley is a reference management tool that helps students organize and annotate their research papers and articles. It allows students to easily import and organize references, create citations and bibliographies, and collaborate with peers on research projects.

- **Fotor AI.** Fotor AI provides students with an extensive range of text and typography customization options. This feature is particularly useful for those working on graphic design and marketing projects, allowing them to create engaging visuals with precise control over fonts, sizes, colors, and styles. It's a valuable resource for students aiming to produce polished and professional-looking design work in their coursework.

- **Stepwise Math.** Stepwise Math is an innovative AI-powered mathematics learning platform designed to assist students in grasping complex mathematical concepts. It offers a guided, step-by-step approach to solving mathematical problems and provides instant feedback on each step of the process. With interactive lessons and practice exercises, Stepwise Math helps students build a solid foundation in math, making it an invaluable tool for those studying mathematics, engineering, physics, or any discipline that requires mathematical proficiency.

- **Google Bard.** Google Bard is a chatbot powered by the PaLm 2 engine, which makes it distinct from ChatGPT. Google Bard is an effective research assistant. While ChatGPT is perhaps best for generating content, Google Bard may excel in analysis and research. Unlike ChatGPT, which is loaded with data from a previous year (at the time of this writing, one year before the current year),

Google Bard uses real-time data. Experiment with combining ChatGPT and Google Bard to get the best perspective on your studies!

- **Slidesgo.** Move over Microsoft Powerpoint! Slidesgo is a versatile online platform that offers a wide range of professionally designed presentation templates, particularly tailored for students, educators, and professionals. This user-friendly resource allows users to create captivating and visually appealing presentations for various purposes, from academic projects and lectures to business proposals and creative pitches.

- **Duolingo.** Many of us have to take language classes in high school and college—it has never been easier with AI. Duolingo, well-known for its language learning platform, serves as a versatile and effective tool that can significantly aid students in their academic pursuits. While primarily designed for language learning, Duolingo offers several features and benefits that extend beyond language acquisition and can play a valuable role in enhancing various aspects of a student's studies.

Best Practices for Using AI Tools to Improve Academic Performance

In this chapter, you may have gotten the impression that academic institutions, quite like many of the rest of us, do not know quite what to make of AI! For the time being, bans of AI for academic purposes seem unlikely or impractical in the long run, even though they have popped up in various school districts currently. So, like the e-reading tools I mentioned in Chapter 1, educators and students ought to get used to the new technology.

The confusion and concern on the part of academic institutions regarding AI is not unwarranted. ChatGPT, to use one example of an AI tool, can easily write a research paper and a term paper. However, are these good papers, or even accurate ones? Moreover, does the AI output represent the intellectual effort of the student? If it does not, is it unethical to use AI to improve your academic performance?

I will answer the first question before I get to the second two.

To understand the limitations of ChatGPT in particular, and AI in general, requires us to have a sense of how this technology works. The reason I described how our brains operate in Chapter 1 is because AI is very much like our brains. This can be viewed after-the-fact in reading ChatGPT's responses to questions. You see, ChatGPT *can* get things wrong, and it predictably gets things wrong in certain domains or areas. When ChatGPT responds to your questions, it's essentially making a very sophisticated and informed *guess*, akin to how our brains decide that getting away from a bear is a better course of action than staying put, or vice versa (depending on whether you think playing dead is better for your survival or not!). A guess, no matter how informed, is still a guess. A guess can lead you to get mauled by a bear. Let me go over an example of when ChatGPT can make an error.

In stating "give me a two-paragraph write-up about hospital management," I get the following response from ChatGPT (emphasis mine):

> Hospital management is a critical component of the healthcare industry, focusing on the effective administration and coordination of medical services, staff, and resources within a hospital or healthcare facility. It plays a pivotal role in ensuring quality patient care, operational efficiency, and compliance with regulatory standards. Effective hospital management often involves strategic planning, financial management, human resource management, and patient satisfaction.
>
> One of the key aspects of hospital management is financial management, which includes budgeting, revenue cycle

management, and cost control. Efficient financial management is crucial to maintaining the financial viability of a hospital. *A study published in the journal "Hospital Topics" by Vukmir and Li, 2020, emphasizes the significance of financial management in healthcare institutions*, highlighting the need for proper budgeting and resource allocation to sustain operations and meet patient demands.

Human resource management is equally vital in the hospital setting. *A study in the "International Journal of Health Policy and Management" by Duygulu and Cirpan, 2018*, discusses the role of human resource management in enhancing healthcare quality and staff satisfaction. Hospital managers need to ensure the recruitment, training, and retention of skilled healthcare professionals while promoting a positive workplace culture. Effective management in this domain can directly impact the overall quality of patient care and the hospital's reputation.

In the version of ChatGPT 3.5 that is used at the time of this writing, the model makes it clear that the citations it uses are placeholders and should not be taken as authoritative. This was less clear in previous versions of the model, and law school students, to use just one example of a potential academic user of ChatGPT, had turned in essays with fabricated case law citations. Here, too, the studies ChatGPT mentions in support of this description of hospital management are fictitious but believable at a brief glance. It is conceivable that these researchers have worked in this field and that these journals mention the topics, but not by those particular authors. When citing work for academic writing, either cite your own resources or do due diligence to ensure that what ChatGPT produces is in line with what would be produced by a human author reviewing the literature.

Now I can return to the remaining two questions I posed at the start of this section on best practices. Basically, is it ethical to use ChatGPT and other AI tools in the production of academic work? Does the work you produce with ChatGPT and other AI tools represent your own?

As it stands now, it is a best practice to cite the use of ChatGPT. It is also a best practice on the part of the academic instructor to make transparent their expectations about the use of ChatGPT and other AI tools in the submission of work. However, standards change for academia and everything else; and, I would like to make an analogy that makes the case that ChatGPT is an ethical tool to use in the production of academic work.

I am old enough to remember the Internet not being a fundamental part of life! During this relative technological stone age, I would often go to the library to do research. A literature review could be conducted in specific libraries related to a field or libraries of any sort. Today, a literature review can be conducted much more effectively using Google Scholar or a similar service. In conducting a literature review, one is transparent about methodology and one states: "I have used Google Scholar to conduct a literature review..." based on certain criteria that one lays out. ChatGPT is the same kind of quantum leap from a brick-and-mortar library to a virtual one. As such, the use of ChatGPT demands acknowledgement but it is beneficial for the same reason the Internet is compared to a brick-and-mortar library.

In my use of ChatGPT for clients and my personal work, I can attest that this tool is exactly that: a tool. A tool can be used to produce what you will, if you are willing to learn the tool. Comparatively, musicians who have made virtual music since the early 2000s have had a variety of software packages at their disposal: FL Studio, Reason, and Logic, to name only three. The music produced from these software packages was not remotely identical between and across them and between and across musicians. Musicians realized that software packages such as those described were instruments of their own. ChatGPT is like an instrument in an orchestra. The orchestra in this case is your life goals, including that of excelling academically.

Academic Integrity

There is no doubt that ChatGPT and other AI tools are a powerful means to succeed academically, with all the caveats I mentioned about checking sources and doing your due diligence. But, how does one reconcile this instrument in your orchestra with academic standards? As I mentioned, the reaction to AI tools on the part of academia has been mixed or inconsistent. Here are some ways to maintain academic integrity when using ChatGPT and other AI tools:

- **Transparency.** As I mentioned, always be transparent about the use of AI tools in your academic work. If you've received assistance or insights from AI, acknowledge it in your work. This includes mentioning the use of AI in the acknowledgments, footnotes, or citations, depending on the academic style required.

- **Proper Attribution.** When AI tools provide specific information or insights, ensure that you attribute the source correctly. This means citing the AI tool or any external sources it references, just as you would with human-authored content.

- **Genuine Effort.** Use AI tools as aids to supplement your academic work, not as replacements for your own critical thinking and research. This is key! The intellectual engagement and understanding of the subject matter should primarily come from you. AI tools can help you find information, generate ideas, and improve your work, but they should not be the sole source of your academic input.

- **Cross-Verification.** As I also stated, make sure to cross-verify the information provided by AI tools with reputable academic sources. It is essential to confirm that the information you're incorporating into your work is accurate and reliable. AI tools can be a valuable starting point, but they should not be the only source you rely on.

- **Academic Policy Adherence.** As much as possible, familiarize yourself with your institution's academic policies and guidelines related to the use of AI tools. Different institutions may have varying stances and rules on their usage. Ensure that you comply with these policies.

- **Educate Yourself.** Take the time to understand how AI tools work and the limitations they may have. This book is only a start! The more you know about the tools you are using, the more empowered you will be to use them effectively and responsibly.

- **Ethical Considerations.** Reflect on the ethical implications of using AI tools in your academic work. Consider how their use may affect your own growth as a learner. After all, you want AI to help you, not compromise the development of your critical thinking, problem-solving skills, and intellectual independence.

Nick's Story

Nick has always struggled in his geography course. For some reason, he couldn't fully retain the concepts and would become totally confused. He couldn't tell the difference between a peninsula from a delta from a plain. His grades suffered. Enter Coursehero. By starting to use this AI study assistant program, Nick was able to get additional explanations about geographic landscapes in YouTube videos, ask questions of experts in this subject matter and even take a few sample tests in preparation for his school exam. Overtime, Nick gained a better understanding of geography and even received an amazing grade on his project making an aquifer model.

By now, I think you have a good sense of the power of AI for your academic career and the do's and don'ts that come with it: namely, *do* due diligence, *don't* depend on AI for everything. But, what about for your actual career? The potential there for AI is even more limitless, as there are typically less restrictions on how you can do your work; there are legal rather than academic restrictions, in other words. If AI can help you get better grades, it can also boost your career! How can we use ChatGPT and other AI tools to do that? Follow me to the next chapter!

Chapter 4: How to Use AI to Boost Your Career

There never hasn't been a time when the job market hasn't been changing—sorry for the triple negative! Perhaps in the European Dark Ages, you knew what to expect day-by-day: your landlord will be your landlord, and you will toil in the fields. Around the time of the Industrial Revolution, things changed because individuals, rather than feudal lords alone, could own property. Suddenly, individuals were empowered to do things in order to pursue their goals and aspirations. For some, their goal was to accumulate more property. For others, their goal was to be craftsmen and artisans. For yet others, it was the beauty of the written word which motivated them. I count myself as among the last category because I am a writer! And, I use my writing ability to support myself and build a career in publishing.

If book publishing was ever a highly-profitable career, this was during a certain era for a certain narrow group of people: think New York, club-going types. It is almost hallucinogenic when you think about what you are doing when you read a book: you are staring at ink on distressed wood for hours at a time to let your imagination fly or to learn something—these days you are possibly reading on a tablet! In any case, I manage to squeak out a living for myself with AI even in book publishing. If you are in any more of a profitable field than this, or wish to be, then I am happy to report to you that the sky is your limit in terms of advancing your career!

Using AI Tools to Update Your Resume

Whatever field you are in—whether it is book publishing or oil drilling or something else—you need to market yourself and you need to stand out: this is the purpose of a resume.

If I reiterate one thing in this book, it is that one ought to adjust their approach to a changing market and a changing market increasingly includes AI. It is inevitable that people will use AI in order to compete with other individuals; we are AI revolutionaries so we are simply among the first to do so!

So, how do we as AI revolutionaries use AI to advertise ourselves within this evolving market? How do we stand out? Here are some ideas for our resumes:

Automated Resume Builders. AI-powered resume builders have revolutionized the way resumes are created. These tools can help you generate a professional and tailored resume by simply inputting your information and preferences. They often offer a variety of templates and formatting options, ensuring your resume looks polished and modern. Multiple automated resume builders, such as Rezi, Kickresume, and Resumaker.ai are available online.

Keyword Optimization. Many companies and recruiters use applicant tracking systems (ATS) to screen resumes. AI tools can analyze job descriptions and suggest keywords that are likely to pass through ATS filters. Integrating these keywords into your resume can increase the chances of it being noticed. Moreover, AI tools can assist you in optimizing the use of these keywords strategically throughout your resume to enhance its visibility and relevance to potential employers, thereby increasing your prospects of landing your desired job.

Customized Content. AI can assist in personalizing your resume for specific job applications. By analyzing the requirements of a job posting and comparing them to your experience, AI can recommend changes to highlight the most relevant skills and accomplishments for each application. Furthermore, AI's ability to tailor your resume for individual job applications, by aligning your qualifications with specific job requirements, can significantly enhance your chances of making a strong impression and securing interviews.

Grammar and Style Checks. AI-driven writing assistants, like Grammarly, can help ensure your resume is free from grammatical errors and stylistic issues. A well-written resume conveys professionalism and attention to detail. Harnessing

AI-driven writing assistants such as Grammarly for grammar and style checks may be pivotal for you in crafting a resume that not only avoids grammatical errors but also exudes a high level of professionalism and meticulous attention to detail.

Data-Backed Insights. AI tools can provide insights into the effectiveness of your resume. They can analyze response rates, interview requests, and other key metrics to help you refine your approach and tailor your resume for better outcomes. Furthermore, AI tools can analyze response rates, interview requests, and other key metrics. This data-driven feedback empowers you to continually refine your approach and tailor your resume for better outcomes in your job search.

Online Presence Enhancement. Increasingly, your online presence is as important as your resume. AI tools can help you optimize your LinkedIn profile, aligning it with your resume for a cohesive professional image. Leveraging AI tools to optimize and harmonize your LinkedIn profile with your resume may be a necessity for you maintaining a coordinated and impactful professional identity.

Skills and Trends Identification. AI tools can help you identify emerging skills and trends in your field. By staying up-to-date with the latest industry requirements, you can ensure your resume reflects your competence in cutting-edge technologies and methodologies. By utilizing AI tools to stay attuned to the ever-evolving skills and trends within your field, you can proactively align your resume with the latest industry demands, showcasing your competence in cutting-edge technologies and methodologies and enhancing your marketability and relevance.

Now, I could go over what makes a good resume, such as detail (this is especially important!), clarity (think: "word economy"), and elegance (or simplicity), but this is not the book for that. Moreover, ChatGPT will tell you everything you need to know about building a resume! It has compiled all of the advice and best practices that I cannot even grasp the theoretical breadth of. In other words, AI can be your trusted companion for spiffing up your resume and landing that dream job. What about boosting productivity when you get that job?

Using AI Tools to Boost Productivity

Meet Melissa: an office worker navigating the fast-paced demands of her career in the bustling heart of her city. Like many other professionals, Melissa's workdays are a whirlwind of meetings, emails, reports, and deadlines. Balancing it all is no small feat, and there were times when Melissa felt the weight of her tasks pressing down on her.

One particularly challenging day, she found herself staring at an overflowing inbox, a to-do list that seemed to grow with every passing hour, and an impending deadline for a critical client presentation.

As the pressure mounted, she realized that she needed a way to boost her productivity and regain control of her workday.

Melissa's story is a familiar one in the modern professional world. The good news is that she, like many others, discovered the transformative power of AI in her career! How did she use AI to boost productivity at her office job? Well, let us go over what she did:

Automated Data Entry. Melissa started by using AI-powered tools to automate data entry tasks. Instead of manually inputting information into spreadsheets or databases, she employed software that could recognize and extract data from various sources, such as scanned documents or emails. This not only saved her time but also reduced the risk of human error.

Email Management. Melissa integrated AI-based email management solutions into her workflow. These tools helped her categorize, prioritize, and even draft responses to emails more efficiently. AI algorithms learned her preferences and habits, allowing for more personalized and effective email organization.

Virtual Assistants. Melissa adopted AI-driven virtual assistants to help with scheduling, reminders, and routine tasks. These virtual assistants could set up meetings, send notifications, and provide quick answers to common queries, reducing the time she spent on administrative duties.

Machine Learning for Research. In her research and data analysis tasks, Melissa utilized machine learning algorithms to sift through vast amounts of data and extract valuable insights. These AI-driven tools helped her make data-driven decisions and improved the accuracy and speed of her research.

Document Management. AI-driven document management systems helped Melissa organize, search, and retrieve documents more efficiently. These systems often used natural language processing to make documents more accessible, saving her the time and frustration of manually sorting through files.

Project Management. To keep track of tasks and projects, Melissa employed AI-powered project management tools. These tools could predict project timelines, allocate resources more effectively, and identify potential bottlenecks, enabling her to better plan and manage her work.

Workflow Automation. Melissa created customized AI workflows to automate repetitive tasks, such as generating reports, sending notifications, or performing routine data analysis. This not only reduced the risk of human error but also freed up her time for more strategic and creative work.

Personalized Learning and Development. AI-driven training platforms tailored to Melissa's needs helped her continuously gain new skills and knowledge relevant to her career. These platforms used adaptive learning algorithms to identify her strengths and weaknesses, ensuring she received the most pertinent training materials.

Voice Assistants. In her daily work routine, Melissa used voice-activated AI assistants to perform tasks hands-free. These assistants could set reminders, make calls, and provide quick answers, enhancing her multitasking abilities.

Data Security. AI-driven security tools helped Melissa protect sensitive data and prevent security breaches. These tools continuously monitored her systems for any suspicious activity and alerted her to potential threats.

I am a bit like Melissa—though less sophisticated! I, too, was able to boost productivity in book publishing through the use of AI. Roughly, I would say I increased my productivity threefold—Melissa increased hers by 10 or 50-fold. I mentioned earlier that the sky is the limit in advancing your career in AI, but what about the jobs that will be displaced with AI? Well, that brings me to another story.

Bryant's Story

Bryant had been a stock trader for over a decade. He had navigated the tumultuous world of finance with a keen eye and a deep understanding of market trends. Moreover, he prided himself on his ability to read the financial tea leaves and make calculated decisions that often resulted in substantial profits for his clients.

However, as the financial industry evolved, so did the role of AI in stock trading. Automated trading algorithms and machine learning models were becoming more sophisticated and efficient, threatening to make traditional human traders like Bryant obsolete. It was a challenging time for many people, and Bryant could sense the changing winds of his career.

Rather than succumb to the fear of AI taking over, however, Bryant decided to embrace the technology and use it to his advantage! He spent months studying and understanding the AI systems that were infiltrating the trading world. He learned about predictive analytics and algorithmic trading strategies. Ultimately, he realized that AI had the potential to be his most powerful tool, not his adversary.

Bryant began integrating AI-driven analysis into his trading strategies. He used AI to sift through vast amounts of data, identify hidden patterns, and make split-second trading decisions that no human could match in speed or accuracy. With his new AI-enhanced approach, he started to make investments that were consistently profitable.

In a remarkable turn of events, Bryant not only secured his job but also saw his profits soar! He was no longer competing with AI; he was partnering with it. His clients were delighted with his newfound success, and he became known as one of the few traders who had successfully adapted to the changing landscape of the financial industry. Bryant's story is a testament to the transformative power of AI when embraced as a tool for advancement rather than a threat to job security.

So, given this case—which I include to show that there is always an avenue for success for us AI revolutionaries in any domain—what jobs are safe and which ones are in danger due to the rise of AI? I turn to that now.

What jobs are safe in the AI revolution and which ones are in danger?

You would think writer is one of them! And, yet, here I am. So, with Bryant and me to show you that there is always an exception to every rule, what jobs are safe and which ones are in danger in the AI revolution?

Jobs Safe in the AI Revolution:

- **Jobs Requiring Creativity.** Professions that involve high levels of creativity, innovation, and emotional intelligence, such as writers, artists, and designers, are less likely to be fully replaced by AI. While AI can assist in these fields, the human touch remains essential for originality and emotional richness—take it from me!

- **Jobs Demanding Critical Thinking.** Roles that rely heavily on complex problem-solving and critical thinking, like research scientists, strategists, and philosophers, are challenging for AI to fully replicate due to the nuanced and context-dependent nature of their work.

- **Jobs Focused on Personal Care.** Occupations providing personal care and emotional support, such as therapists, counselors, and healthcare providers, inherently require human empathy, understanding, and emotional connection that AI cannot replicate.

- **Jobs in Skilled Trades.** Skilled trades such as plumbing, carpentry, and electrician work involve hands-on problem-solving and adaptability to unique situations, making them less susceptible to automation.

Jobs at Risk in the AI Revolution:

- **Repetitive and Manual Tasks.** Jobs that primarily involve repetitive and manual tasks, like assembly line workers, data entry clerks, and some administrative roles, are at higher risk of automation.

- **Basic Customer Service.** Basic customer service positions, especially those involving routine inquiries or simple problem-solving, can be automated through chatbots and virtual assistants.

- **Data Analysis and Entry.** Roles that predominantly consist of data analysis and entry may face automation as AI can process and analyze vast datasets more efficiently.

- **Transportation and Delivery.** With advancements in autonomous vehicles and drones, jobs in transportation and delivery, such as truck drivers and couriers, may be affected by automation.

You may recall that Melissa, the office worker who utilized AI to assist in her career, automated much of the data analysis and entry she would have otherwise done personally. She also automated logistics and delivery in terms of email communication, and she automated customer service processes for her company. Finally, she switched out some administrative jobs for AI.

What is the news for Melissa? Well, Melissa is getting paid—probably more than she was before! I can attest I am getting paid more than I was before thanks to AI. Anyways, some people *like* these anecdotes, but others are less enamored by them. Let's take a look at how AI is affecting job markets and decide if the anecdotes fit the greater trends.

How AI is Impacting Unpredictable Job Markets

In the introduction, I talked about how AI is impacting job markets: by both displacing jobs and providing opportunities for innovation and retraining. To summarize what I stated there, jobs that require automated processes (including manual labor) are most at risk of being displaced by AI, whereas creative jobs (including mine as a writer!) are relatively safer. Emil Skandul (2023), writing for *Business Insider*, repeats the insight of many of other commentators on AI and the unpredictable job market: "AI is going to eliminate way more jobs than anyone realizes," he claims, yet "nongenerative and generative AI are estimated to add between $17 trillion and $26 trillion to the global economy. And crucially, many of the jobs that will be lost will be replaced by new ones."

Indeed, Skandul (2023) is correct when he writes that AI is "likely to be a transformation as influential as the industrial revolution and the rise of the internet. The changes could boost living standards, improve productivity, and accelerate economic opportunities, but this rosy future is not guaranteed." What is not guaranteed is the success of AI on a public level and on your own personal level. How do you test if your job is safe during the AI revolution? Moreover, how do you use AI to promote your business or products? These are the topics of the rest of the chapter.

How To Test if Your Job is Safe During the AI Revolution

Sometimes I feel like working with AI is like boarding a spaceship! It really is that futuristic—but in a more subtle way. I've found my work readily improved with the use of AI, but it is still my work. As I mentioned in the last chapter, AI has simply become an instrument in the orchestra that is my life. Still, I know you may feel unsettled: the question of job security during the AI revolution looms large, even for a revolutionary! Here are some factors to consider for whether your job can be guarded from displacement during the AI revolution:

- **Level of Automation.** Evaluate the degree to which your job relies on automated processes. Jobs involving highly repetitive and rule-based tasks are more susceptible to automation. If your role primarily involves such activities, it might be at a higher risk of displacement by AI. Conversely, if your job requires creativity, problem-solving, or interpersonal skills, it may be less vulnerable.

- **Adaptability.** Consider your willingness and ability to adapt to changes in your industry. Jobs that can evolve alongside technology and harness AI as a tool for efficiency and innovation are better positioned for longevity. A commitment to continuous learning and staying updated with industry trends can be a valuable asset.

- **Interdisciplinary Skills.** Explore opportunities to broaden your skill set. The ability to work at the intersection of different disciplines can make you more resilient to automation. For instance, combining technical expertise with creativity or business acumen can open up new career paths.

- **Human Interaction.** Assess the extent to which your job requires human interaction and emotional intelligence. AI struggles to replicate the nuanced aspects of human connection and empathy. Roles that involve counseling, coaching, healthcare, and other human-centric fields are less likely to be automated.

- **Research and Anticipation**. Stay informed about AI developments in your industry and anticipate potential changes. Understanding how AI is being integrated can help you proactively adapt and position yourself for job security.

Schedule Planning

One way to boost productivity at work is to better plan your time and commitments. This approach will lead to a healthier you overall, as I discuss in Chapter 9. Check out the following AI apps to optimize your time in and outside of work (Rebelo, 2023):

Reclaim.ai. Reclaim.ai stands out as a versatile application that seamlessly merges scheduling with productivity optimization by offering a harmonious balance between work and personal life, particularly for those adopting a hybrid or remote work model. Users attests to the utility of tools like Reclaim in analyzing work habits and fine-tuning schedules for an improved work-life equilibrium. Reclaim.ai can recommend effective time management strategies, allocate breaks, and prevent calendar overload.

Clockwise. Clockwise is a fantastic tool for syncing team calendars. Its intelligent algorithms simplify the process of scheduling meetings, allowing teams to coordinate seamlessly. By analyzing everyone's schedules, it ensures that meetings are arranged at the most convenient times, reducing scheduling conflicts and making the most of available time.

Motion. Motion is a game-changer for AI-assisted project management. It optimizes project workflows by leveraging AI to identify bottlenecks, forecast potential issues, and provide real-time insights. This proactive approach allows teams to address problems before they become significant roadblocks, enhancing project efficiency and ensuring deadlines are met.

Clara. Clara introduces a remarkable human-like AI virtual assistant to the workplace. With its natural language processing capabilities, Clara can efficiently manage emails, appointments, and even schedule meetings, often leaving users wondering if they're interacting with a human! This level of AI sophistication can significantly enhance productivity and streamline daily administrative tasks.

Trevor. Trevor, the simple yet powerful AI solution for task management, caters to users who value a straightforward approach. Offering free and accessible task management, it helps individuals and teams stay organized and productive. Trevor's intuitive interface makes it easy for users to create, prioritize, and track tasks, enhancing overall efficiency.

Kronologic. Kronologic is a valuable resource for sales and marketing teams, as it excels at following up with more leads. It streamlines lead nurturing by using AI-driven scheduling and reminders to ensure that leads are not forgotten or left to languish. By automating this process, Kronologic helps businesses engage more effectively with potential clients, resulting in increased conversion rates.

Todoist. Task management becomes streamlined with Todoist, an application designed for efficient task organization and creating impactful to-do lists. Todoist can help you organize your days, keeping track of tasks, saving time, and enhancing overall efficiency in day-to-day life. Todoist's user-friendly interface and flexibility make it a versatile tool that caters to a wide range of users, from students and professionals to busy parents.

Scheduler AI. Scheduler AI is a fantastic solution for managing meetings in busy teams. It removes the hassle of scheduling by allowing users to share their availability with the AI. Scheduler AI then arranges meetings after taking everyone's preferences into account. This efficient approach reduces the back-and-forth associated with scheduling, saving time and keeping teams on track and focused on their core task.

How to Market Your Business or Products Using AI

Perhaps a view of job displacement as being related to AI is the wrong one! For me, AI has been a supplement or tool: an instrument. My job has not been displaced; it only skyrocketed in its profitability. So, despite these doom-and-gloom predictions about AI and job displacement, why not use AI for our benefits? It clearly works to help us get better grades and improve our productivity at work—if not get new jobs entirely! So, if we can market ourselves to employers using AI, how do we use AI to market our business or products to the general public?

Well, when it comes to marketing your business or products to the general public, AI offers a multitude of strategies for success:

Data-driven marketing. AI's prowess in analyzing consumer data is nothing short of a game-changer for modern businesses. By sifting through vast datasets, AI can uncover intricate trends, preferences, and behavior patterns that might otherwise remain hidden. This valuable information provides a deeper understanding of your audience's needs and desires, allowing you to fine-tune your marketing strategies to an unprecedented degree.

With AI's insights, you can develop a laser-focused approach to tailor your products and messages. For instance, you can identify specific consumer segments with distinct preferences and create customized marketing campaigns that resonate with each group. This level of personalization not only boosts the relevance of your offerings but also cultivates a deeper connection between your brand and the consumer.

Moreover, AI's data-driven analysis empowers you to adapt swiftly to changing market dynamics. As trends evolve and consumer behavior shifts, AI can detect these shifts in real-time, enabling you to make timely adjustments to your strategies. This agility is a critical advantage in a rapidly changing business landscape, ensuring that you remain competitive and responsive to your audience's evolving demands.

Personalized Recommendations. AI's remarkable proficiency in analyzing consumer data represents a monumental leap forward for contemporary businesses. As it delves into vast and intricate datasets, AI has the uncanny ability to unveil hidden trends, discern subtle preferences, and decode complex behavior patterns. The insights drawn from this wealth of information offer businesses a profound understanding of their audience's needs and desires, allowing for the meticulous refinement of marketing strategies to an unparalleled degree of precision.

With AI as your guiding hand, you can craft a finely-tuned approach that tailors your products and messaging to a degree of detail previously thought unattainable. For instance, AI enables the identification of specific consumer segments characterized by unique preferences. This newfound knowledge empowers businesses to create marketing campaigns that are not only customized but resonate deeply with each distinct group. This level of personalization not only enhances the pertinence of your product offerings but also nurtures a profound connection between your brand and the consumer, fostering brand loyalty and trust.

Furthermore, AI's data-driven analysis provides a dynamic and adaptive edge in an ever-evolving market. As trends morph and consumer behavior undergoes shifts, AI stands vigilant in real-time detection of these transformations, granting you the ability to promptly adjust your strategies. This agility is a pivotal asset in a business landscape marked by rapid change, ensuring that you remain both competitive and responsive to the evolving demands of your audience.

Chatbots and Virtual Assistants. AI-driven chatbots represent an invaluable asset for delivering instantaneous customer support, addressing inquiries, and shepherding customers through the intricacies of the purchasing journey. These tireless bots are accessible around the clock, resulting in significant enhancements in customer satisfaction and notable upswings in conversion rates.

By seamlessly engaging with customers at any hour, AI-powered chatbots eliminate the constraints of time zones and business hours, thereby ensuring a round-the-clock, uninterrupted avenue for customers to seek assistance. This unfettered accessibility is a game-changer in customer service, obliterating the frustrations associated with delayed responses and extended waiting times.

The impact on customer satisfaction is unmistakable. The immediate availability of support, the ability to swiftly resolve queries, and the seamless guidance provided by chatbots all contribute to a heightened sense of customer contentment. This not only results in increased loyalty but also prompts positive word-of-mouth recommendations, effectively becoming a catalyst for business growth.

Moreover, the efficiency and swiftness of AI-driven chatbots translate into tangible results on conversion rates. By addressing potential customer concerns promptly and facilitating a frictionless purchasing process, these chatbots significantly reduce the risk of cart abandonment and contribute to an uptick in completed transactions.

Content Creation. Harness AI to produce marketing content, spanning from informative blog posts to captivating product descriptions and engaging social media updates. AI's contribution to content creation is undeniably valuable, streamlining the process and ensuring a consistent output of high-quality material. However, it is paramount to strike a delicate balance, as preserving the human touch guarantees authenticity.

AI excels in generating content swiftly and efficiently, drawing from extensive data sources and adapting to specific tones or styles. It can effortlessly create large volumes of content, catering to various platforms and target audiences. This capability not only saves time but also ensures that your marketing efforts maintain a consistent and frequent presence, a crucial factor in today's fast-paced digital landscape.

Nonetheless, the human element is indispensable in maintaining the authenticity and relatability of the content. AI may craft well-structured text, but it might lack the nuanced creativity, emotion, and cultural understanding that a human touch brings. Therefore, while AI can be a valuable tool for content creation, human oversight and editing are vital to ensure that the content resonates with the intended audience.

Predictive Analytics. Harness the potential of AI-driven predictive analytics to forecast demand, optimize inventory management, and fine-tune pricing strategies. This data-driven approach is instrumental in not only meeting customer expectations but also maximizing profitability.

AI's predictive analytics have the capability to analyze historical data, market trends, and consumer behavior to make accurate forecasts about future demand. By understanding what products or services are likely to be in high demand, you can ensure that your inventory is well-prepared to meet customer needs. This prevents stockouts and overstock situations, ultimately leading to cost savings and improved customer satisfaction.

Efficient inventory management also extends to the reduction of carrying costs and the minimization of waste, as you can precisely stock items based on anticipated demand. This level of precision contributes to streamlining your operations, improving resource allocation, and increasing overall efficiency.

Moreover, AI-driven predictive analytics aids in optimizing pricing strategies. By considering factors like supply and demand, competitor pricing, and consumer behavior, AI can suggest the most competitive and profitable price points for your products or services. This ensures that you remain both attractive to customers and profitable, striking the ideal balance that drives business growth.

Voice Search Optimization. As the use of voice-activated devices continues to surge in popularity, it becomes imperative to optimize your online content for voice search. AI plays a pivotal role in tailoring your content to seamlessly accommodate voice search queries, ensuring that your digital presence remains relevant and accessible in this evolving landscape.

Voice-activated devices, such as smart speakers and virtual assistants, have transformed the way people seek information online. Rather than typing keyword-heavy queries, users now employ conversational language when making voice searches. AI steps in as a valuable ally in deciphering these natural language queries and adapting your content accordingly.

By incorporating AI-driven optimization, your online content becomes attuned to the nuances of voice search. This enables your content to respond effectively to voice-activated queries, increasing its visibility and relevance to a broader audience. As a result, you not only keep pace with changing consumer behavior but also enhance the user experience—ultimately improving your online presence and engagement with a rapidly growing voice-search user base.

In summary, in this chapter, I showed how you can harness the power of AI to find and secure jobs, improve your productivity at work with AI, and market your business or products using AI. I hope you have a good sense of what AI can do for you in the broad strokes of your career! Now, let us look at one aspect of business where AI can seamlessly integrate: social media.

Social media has been called many things: from a boon to a scourge. What it has never been called is unprofitable—ah, a double negative, this time! Please follow me, dear reader, to the next chapter where I outline how you can use AI to uncover the myriad business opportunities on social media.

Chapter 5: How to Use AI for Social Media Opportunities

Thank you, dear reader, for making it this far in *The AI Success Route*! I hope, by now, you feel empowered to utilize AI for the purposes of improving your studies and career. Yet, there are many other uses for AI: among these are making money on social media and improving your social life. The rest of this book is dedicated to exploring the many other uses of AI to better your life.

I left off the last chapter by stating that social media has been considered a boon or a scourge depending on who you ask. In reality, social media is a new normal! Much like AI increasingly is. However you look at social media, though, there is plenty of money to be made on it, and AI will increasingly play a critical role in harvesting the business opportunities from social media.

But, how does AI facilitate discovering and making good from these opportunities? This is the topic of this chapter.

Business opportunities on social media can be divided into three general categories: customer analysis, content creation, and social media marketing. Let us look at each individually.

Customer Analysis on Social Media

What do you know about social media analysis used on sites like Facebook, LinkedIn, Twitter (now X), and Instagram? Well, social media analysis generally encompasses the extraction of information and insights from the vast expanse of data found on social media platforms. On the Internet, we all leave behind a trace of communication and these traces form a profile for us. With these profiles, businesses can target advertisements and content directly to those who would engage with it most.

Now, social media analysis typically entails the examination of extensive user-generated content. This content spans posts, comments, images, and videos, and it is across a diverse array of social media platforms. The conventional approach of manually analyzing social media data is extremely time-consuming; it typically involves Excel spreadsheets and SQL databases and the like. Here, AI-powered solutions have emerged as a transformative force because they provide automated and scalable techniques to effectively manage extensive data sets and extract meaningful insights.

A common way AI is used for studying social media is through something called *sentiment analysis*. In this process, AI algorithms are used to automatically figure out whether social media posts express positive, negative, or neutral feelings. The idea is that by looking at these sentiments related to specific products, brands, or topics, companies can gain useful insights into what customers like or think about them.

Then, this knowledge can subsequently guide marketing tactics, product enhancements, and customer service endeavors. For example, a restaurant chain may employ social media sentiment analysis to grasp customer reactions to their menu offerings. This enables the restaurant to make informed choices geared toward enhancing customer satisfaction.

AI-driven social monitoring tools empower companies to oversee and scrutinize discussions occurring on social media concerning their brand, offerings, or specific industry. These tools make use of natural language processing (NLP) algorithms to detect and classify pertinent social media posts, references, and hashtags. Through the tracking and examination of these dialogues, companies can enhance their comprehension of customer requirements, sentiments, and prevailing patterns. Social monitoring aids companies in pinpointing emerging concerns: it promptly addresses customer issues and even recognizes the prospects for novelty or promotional campaigns. For example, an e-commerce firm can observe social media conversations to pinpoint trending product preferences and adjust its inventory accordingly.

AI-driven *visual analysis* stands as another compelling facet of social media analysis. As visual content gains escalating prominence across social media platforms, companies can harness AI to derive invaluable perspectives from images and videos. For instance, image recognition algorithms can scrutinize images to pinpoint brand logos, products, or gauge customer sentiments by interpreting facial expressions. In parallel, *video analysis* can uncover trends, prevailing subjects, and the sentiments conveyed within video content. This extensive exploration of visual content empowers businesses to attain a more profound insight into customer predilections and, in turn, refine their marketing strategies accordingly.

Comprehending the competitive environment holds significant importance for businesses of all kinds, and this environment is evident on social media. AI offers the means to scrutinize data from social media to open a window into the strategies, audience interaction, and sentiment of competitors. By monitoring the social media endeavors of rivals, businesses can uncover prospects, measure their own performance against benchmarks, and adapt their social media strategies in response. The utilization of AI for *competitive analysis* delivers an all-encompassing perspective of the market, and it enables businesses to maintain a competitive edge in their field.

Assessing the success of social media campaigns is a crucial step in gauging the return on investment and guiding data-driven choices for subsequent campaigns. AI technologies come into play here by scrutinizing social media indicators like engagement, reach, and conversions to assess how well campaigns are performing. Through the use of AI-driven analytical tools, companies can attain more profound understandings regarding the effectiveness of their campaigns, recognize aspects that require enhancement, and fine-tune their strategies for social media marketing.

A/B testing is another widely used method in social media advertising that involves evaluating the effectiveness of various ad versions. AI comes into play by automating the A/B testing process, sifting through ad performance data, and uncovering patterns and trends. AI algorithms have the capability to pinpoint which ad variations outperform others by drawing on metrics like click-through rates, conversions, and engagement. This process aids businesses in fine-tuning their ad campaigns, ensuring efficient budget allocation, and maximizing the return on their ad expenditure.

Finally, *data visualization* holds a crucial position in grasping intricate social media data and conveying it in a visually engaging and significant manner. AI-driven data visualization applications have the capacity to assess social media data and craft interactive visual representations, charts, and graphs that simplify the interpretation and communication of insights. Through AI, businesses can fabricate user-friendly dashboards and reports that allow stakeholders to swiftly comprehend significant social media trends and metrics.

Content Generation on Social Media

Creating captivating and relevant content is an essential pillar of successful social media marketing, as I discussed when I mentioned content generation in the last chapter. In an age where information flows rapidly and attention spans are limited, the ability to engage and resonate with your target audience through well-crafted content can make a substantial difference in your bottom line. This ambition is where AI-driven technologies come into play and provide businesses with a competitive edge.

AI technologies, such as NLP and machine learning, possess the capability to analyze vast volumes of data from various sources. These data encompasses a wide spectrum of content, including social media posts, articles, comments, and more. Through this analysis, AI can uncover valuable insights that serve as the bedrock of content creation and strategy optimization.

One of the primary benefits of AI in content creation is its ability to identify trends and emerging topics.

By scanning through extensive datasets, AI can recognize patterns in discussions, pinpoint hot topics, and predict what is likely to gain traction in the near future. This information is what allows businesses to stay ahead of the curve and helps them keep their content fresh and relevant.

Furthermore, AI can assist in content personalization. By examining user interactions and preferences, AI can recommend content that is more likely to resonate with individual users. This level of personalization enhances the user experience and fosters a deeper connection between the brand and the consumer.

Finally, AI-driven chatbots have revolutionized customer support in the era of digital technology, as I also spoke about when I mentioned chatbots in the previous chapter. Numerous companies have adopted chatbots across social media channels to offer immediate support and aid to their clientele. These chatbots harness AI and natural language processing methods to comprehend customer inquiries, furnish pertinent information, and resolve typical problems. Through the integration of chatbots into social media platforms, businesses can provide round-the-clock customer support, enhance response times, and elevate customer contentment. Chatbots are adept at managing a broad spectrum of queries, and they encompass tasks such as order tracking, dispensing product details, and tackling basic troubleshooting—thus affording human agents the liberty to focus on more pressing customer issues.

AI Marketing on Social Media

When we market our enterprises, we are always trying to stay ahead of the curve—in fact, we are trying to predict the next curve. This "staying ahead" is what economists call *jumping the s-curve*: the discovery of new markets to keep your business competitive. AI has never been more crucial to this endeavor!

Predictive analytics is a crucial method to assist in marketing: both identifying who to market to and how to market to them. AI-driven predictive analytics empowers companies to forecast customer behavior, trends, and inclinations by harnessing social media data. AI may be the closest we will get to seeing the future in terms of marketing our products!

The foundation of predictive analytics lies in the careful examination of historical social media data, coupled with insights from various other data sources. This holistic approach allows predictive analytics models based in AI to uncover patterns, detect recurring trends, and foresee future developments. This information, often hidden within the vast sea of data, is like a treasure trove for businesses who are seeking to optimize their social media marketing strategies. These data are also what allow businesses to make informed decisions that boost their bottom line.

Insights from predictive analytics aids businesses in fine-tuning their social media marketing tactics; it allows for the pinpointing of particular customer segments and the crafting of content designed to enhance engagement to the fullest. For instance, a fashion label can employ predictive analytics to determine the prevailing fashion trends most favored by its target demographic and devise precision-targeted marketing campaigns to endorse relevant products.

Predictive analytics is not just about looking at past data; it is about peering into the future, as much as possible, and making informed decisions. This forward-thinking approach equips businesses and individuals with the tools they need to adapt swiftly to changing customer preferences and to tailor their marketing strategies for maximum impact. With predictive analytics, you can navigate the ever-evolving landscape of social media marketing with confidence and finesse. This ensures, also as much as possible, that your content is not just heard but truly resonates with your audience.

In recent years, *influencer marketing* has experienced a notable surge in popularity as a means for businesses to efficiently connect with their desired audience. AI-driven algorithms offer the means to detect and assess social media influencers using criteria like the number of followers, engagement levels, and the relevance of their content. By employing AI for influencer identification, businesses can locate the appropriate influencers who share their brand values and possess a genuine rapport with their intended audience. This empowers them to establish genuine partnerships and execute effective influencer marketing initiatives. Additionally, AI tools can monitor the performance of influencer campaigns, delivering insights on their reach, engagement, and return on investment.

Best AI Tools for Social Media Management

Maintaining a consistent online presence is a crucial factor in achieving success on social media platforms. The ability to regularly deliver high-quality content each week not only satisfies the algorithms but also ensures your brand reaches a wider audience. However, the process of content creation, managing posting schedules, and determining what resonates with your audience can be quite challenging—even with the assistance of conventional social media management tools.

Miguel Rebelo (2023), writing for *Zapier*, uncovers eight crucial AI tools for social media management which solve many of the difficulties of this process outlined in this chapter. I expand on his list:
- **FeedHive** is a valuable tool for repurposing and strategically scheduling your content. It

helps you make the most of your existing materials and ensures your posts are shared at optimal times.

- **Vista Social** serves as a hub for linking numerous social media channels, simplifying your online presence management by providing a centralized platform for your diverse social networks.

- **Buffer** is an essential asset for organizing and executing your posting schedules. It empowers you to plan and launch post campaigns efficiently and effectively.

- **Flick** takes your content ideas and amplifies them, enabling you to create multiple engaging posts from a single concept. It's a fantastic tool for enhancing your content strategy.

- **Audiense** is your go-to solution for intelligent social listening on Twitter. It allows you to tap into trending topics and keep a pulse on your audience's sentiments.

- **Ocoya** is your companion for crafting compelling captions and hashtags, ensuring your posts are well-optimized for visibility and engagement.

- **Predis.ai** simplifies the process of generating captivating carousels and videos, making your content more engaging and shareable.

- **Publer** is the ideal tool for generating post content and visuals, making it easier to maintain a consistent and appealing social media presence.

- ***ContentStudio*** is your key to staying informed and up-to-date on a wide range of content topics, helping you maintain an authoritative and relevant online presence.

- **Taplio** is the perfect partner for building and expanding your personal brand on LinkedIn, helping you connect with your professional network effectively.

- **Hootsuite** enhances your posting diversity through AI-assisted post suggestions, ensuring your content remains fresh and engaging for your audience.

Social media is a new normal and AI is yet another one! It is only natural that the two forces are combined to harness the power of each: our interconnectedness and the traces we leave on the Internet with the transformative ability of AI supercomputations. I bet you can imagine a whole host of horrible outcomes that this intersection of social media and AI can lead to: political manipulation being one. But, it can also lead to your business' success if you harness the power of social media and AI appropriately! With the tools and techniques you learned in this chapter, everything from social media analytics to influencer marketing will be a breeze.

In this chapter, I discussed how to harness AI for social media opportunities. Here, I also described how AI can revolutionize your approach to engaging with your audience and optimizing your marketing strategies. But, AI's transformative capabilities extend far beyond social media alone! Venture with me to the next chapter where you will unlock the potential of AI in another domain: creating a lucrative side hustle. There, you will discover how AI can be your secret weapon in identifying new income streams, automating business processes, and uncovering unexplored opportunities to turn your skills and passions into a profitable venture. So, let us embark on the next stage of the journey, where we will bridge the gap between the innovative world of AI in social media and the prospects that await us with AI-powered side hustles in *The AI Success Route*.

Chapter 6: How to Use AI to Create a Lucrative Side Hustle

About 1/3rd of our lives are spent at work (Gettysburg College, 2023). It is for this reason that we are often told to do what we love! Then, we wouldn't have to work a day in our lives, right?

In reality, we often have careers that we tolerate or even dislike. That is just the reality of it! We are always on the lookout for new opportunities: in the last chapter, these opportunities were on social media. There, I showed you how to use AI to benefit from networks of people who are exposed to your products or services. In this chapter, business opportunities are everywhere, many of which are also online! AI gives you the ability to generate money through a lucrative side hustle. Here, I describe how this is done.

Some Ideas for Your AI-Assisted Side Hustle

Have you finished integrating AI into your career and studies and want another application for this revolutionary technology? Below are some ideas to transform AI into a lucrative side hustle:

AI-Powered Freelancing Programs. One of the most accessible ways to kickstart a side hustle with AI is by leveraging freelancing platforms. These platforms, such as Upwork, Freelancer, and Fiverr, offer a wealth of opportunities for individuals with AI-related skills. Whether you are adept at machine learning, data analysis, content generation, or any other AI domain, you can find clients seeking your expertise. AI can help you streamline your work, making tasks more efficient and potentially more profitable. For instance, AI tools can assist in automating repetitive data analysis or content creation, allowing you to take on more projects and increase your earnings.

In addition to freelancing platforms, another promising way to kickstart a side hustle with AI is through creating and marketing AI-driven products or services. With a growing interest in AI across various industries, there is a demand for innovative solutions. You can develop AI-powered apps, chatbots, or analytical tools and market them to businesses or individuals looking to enhance their operations. This approach not only allows you to showcase your AI skills but it also has the potential for long-term scalability and revenue growth. Building a unique, AI-based product can set you apart and provide you a source of passive income while you continue to freelance or work on other projects.

Content Generation. As I mentioned in previous chapters, AI-driven content generation tools have evolved significantly in recent years. These tools can create high-quality articles, blog posts, product descriptions, and more! You can capitalize on this technology to offer content writing services to businesses in need of consistent, well-written content for their websites and marketing efforts. AI can help you produce content faster and more efficiently, which can lead to higher earnings and better use of your time.

Furthermore, when offering AI-driven content writing services, it is important to remember that AI is a valuable assistant rather than a replacement for human creativity and expertise. While AI can generate well-structured content, your role as a content creator goes beyond just words on a page. You can curate content with a unique voice, inject creativity, and tailor it to the specific needs and preferences of your clients. This personal touch and understanding of client objectives will set you apart in the market, and it makes your content services even more valuable. It is the combination of AI's efficiency and your creative input that can make your content writing business thrive in the digital age.

E-Commerce Optimization. If you are considering an e-commerce side hustle, AI can be your best friend! AI-powered tools can help you optimize product listings, pricing, and even customer support. For instance, AI can analyze market trends and competition to recommend competitive prices, suggest product bundling, and even automate responses to customer inquiries. This efficiency can make your e-commerce side hustle more profitable and manageable.

Additionally, AI can greatly enhance the customer experience in your e-commerce side hustle. Chatbots and virtual assistants powered by AI can provide immediate assistance to customers, answering common questions, guiding them through the purchase process, and offering personalized product recommendations. This not only improves customer satisfaction but also frees up your time to focus on other aspects of your side hustle, such as sourcing new products or marketing. The ability to offer round-the-clock support, thanks to AI, can also help build trust with your customers and ultimately contribute to the success of your e-commerce venture.

AI-Powered Chatbots. As I mentioned in this and previous chapters, AI chatbots have revolutionized customer support, and you can use them to your advantage. Many businesses are seeking chatbot developers to enhance their customer service capabilities. You can offer chatbot development services and integrate AI-powered chatbots into your clients' websites or messaging platforms. This not only provides a valuable solution to businesses but also opens up opportunities for a profitable side hustle.

Furthermore, as the adoption of AI chatbots continues to grow, you can expand your side hustle by offering customization and advanced features. Businesses often have unique needs for their customer support, and your expertise can help tailor chatbots to their specific requirements. You can develop chatbots that can handle complex customer inquiries, provide detailed product information, or even assist in appointment scheduling. By staying up-to-date with the latest AI advancements and continuously improving your chatbot offerings, you can ensure that your services remain in high demand, creating a thriving and dynamic side hustle in the AI chatbot development industry.

Social Media Management. As I described in the last chapter, AI can make managing social media accounts more efficient! You can offer social media management services to businesses looking to boost their online presence. AI tools can help schedule posts, analyze engagement, and even suggest content ideas. By using AI to streamline your social media management tasks, you can handle more clients and increase your income.

Moreover, your expertise in AI-powered social media management can extend beyond scheduling and analysis. Businesses are constantly seeking innovative ways to stand out on social platforms. You can leverage AI to implement targeted advertising campaigns, harness predictive analytics to identify the best posting times, and even use sentiment analysis to gauge the effectiveness of their content. As the demand for comprehensive social media strategies continues to grow, offering these advanced AI-driven services can set you apart in the market and provide your side hustle with the potential for significant growth and client retention.

Data Analysis and Insights. With the growing importance of data-driven decision-making, businesses are constantly seeking professionals who can interpret and analyze data. AI can assist in data analysis, making it easier to uncover valuable insights. Whether this involves market research, customer behavior analysis, or financial data evaluation, offering data analysis services can be a lucrative side hustle with AI.

Furthermore, the application of AI in data analysis is not limited to automating routine tasks but also includes the development of sophisticated predictive models and data visualization tools. As a data analyst, you can leverage AI to offer advanced services such as predictive analytics, anomaly detection, and machine learning model development. These services can help businesses make more accurate forecasts, identify emerging trends, and optimize their strategies. By staying current with the latest AI advancements in data analysis, you can position yourself as an invaluable resource for businesses looking to harness the power of data for better decision-making, thereby expanding the opportunities and profitability of your AI-driven data analysis side hustle.

Online Education. If you are knowledgeable in a field or industry, you can create online courses or tutorials. AI can help you personalize the learning experience for your students, offer automated quizzes and assessments, and even provide recommendations for further study. Online education is a growing industry, and your expertise can turn into a profitable side hustle with AI.

In addition to creating online courses and tutorials, you can use AI to enhance the scalability and effectiveness of your educational offerings. AI-powered chatbots and virtual assistants can provide immediate responses to student queries, ensuring a smooth learning experience. Furthermore, machine learning algorithms can analyze students' progress and tailor the content delivery to their individual needs. This personalized approach not only increases student engagement but also results in higher satisfaction and retention rates, thereby making your online courses more attractive in the competitive online education landscape. As the demand for online learning continues to rise, your side hustle in creating AI-enhanced educational content can become a reliable source of income and personal fulfillment.

Google Ads Manager. Utilizing AI to manage Google Ads campaigns can be a highly profitable side hustle. AI tools can optimize ad spend, target specific demographics, and refine keyword strategies, ensuring clients get the best return on investment. The competition can be high, but with the right expertise and AI tools, you can excel in this lucrative field.

Additionally, as businesses increasingly recognize the need for data-driven marketing strategies, you can offer more comprehensive AI-driven marketing services beyond Google Ads. AI can enable you to analyze customer behavior, segment audiences, and develop highly targeted advertising campaigns across various platforms. This broader approach allows you to provide a holistic digital marketing solution to your clients, ensuring their online presence is well-optimized and their advertising strategies are aligned with their goals. By leveraging AI to offer a suite of marketing services, you can position your side hustle as an indispensable partner for businesses looking to navigate the dynamic and competitive digital marketing landscape, thereby expanding your opportunities and profitability.

Digital Advertising Consultancy. Offering digital advertising consultancy services backed by AI tools can be a profitable side hustle with moderate competition. AI-driven analytics can help clients refine their advertising strategies, improve targeting, and boost ROI. Leveraging AI in consultancy services can set you apart in a competitive market.

Furthermore, as AI continues to advance, your digital advertising consultancy services can evolve to provide innovative solutions to clients! AI can be instrumental in implementing emerging advertising technologies, such as programmatic advertising and AI-powered chatbots for customer engagement. Staying up-to-date with these cutting-edge tools and techniques enables you to offer unique and tailored solutions, which provides you with a competitive advantage in the market. By showcasing your ability to adapt to the ever-changing digital advertising landscape and maximize the potential of AI-driven strategies, you can establish a lucrative side hustle with a growing and diverse client base.

AI-Enhanced Web Development. Building AI-enhanced websites and web applications for businesses is a high-potential side hustle. AI can enhance user experiences, automate customer service, and improve website functionality. With many small businesses seeking affordable AI solutions, this niche offers room for growth.

Moreover, in the realm of AI-enhanced web development, there is an opportunity to create and offer AI-powered plugins or modules that can be integrated into existing websites. For instance, you can develop chatbots, recommendation engines, or AI-driven search functionalities that businesses can easily incorporate into their web platforms. These ready-made AI solutions not only save businesses time and resources but also provide an additional revenue stream for your side hustle. By combining your web development skills with AI expertise and creating versatile, customizable AI modules, you can establish a robust and sustainable business catering to the growing demand for AI-enhanced web solutions.

AI Tutoring. Leveraging AI to offer AI or machine learning tutoring services can be a niche with low competition and a high potential for growth. Many students and professionals seek to upskill in AI, and personalized tutoring with AI tools can set you apart.

Additionally, when providing AI or machine learning tutoring services, you have the flexibility to tailor your offerings to a diverse range of learners. From beginners looking to grasp the fundamentals to experienced practitioners aiming to tackle complex AI projects, your expertise and personalized guidance can cater to various skill levels and objectives. This adaptability not only enhances the value you bring to your clients but it also widens your client base. Whether you prepare students for AI certification exams or help professionals address specific industry challenges, your AI tutoring side hustle can offer a dynamic and continually expanding range of services, opening up opportunities for sustained growth.

AI-Generated Design and Artwork. AI-generated art and design services can be a unique and creative side hustle. Using AI for art generation or design can lead to one-of-a-kind creations, which may attract a niche market willing to pay for exclusive pieces.

Furthermore, the use of AI-generated art and design allows you to explore unconventional and cutting-edge concepts, making your side hustle stand out in a crowded creative landscape. AI can assist in generating art that is often contemporary and innovative, which appeals to those who appreciate the intersection of technology and creativity. Finally, AI tools can facilitate the rapid production of diverse artworks or designs by offering clients a wide range of options to choose from. With the potential for customization, you can create pieces tailored to individual preferences with a level of personalization that is often hard to achieve through traditional means. This creative flexibility, combined with the uniqueness of AI-generated art, can attract a niche market willing to invest in original, AI-crafted works, providing a distinctive and promising avenue for your side hustle.

So, do you think you have enough to get started on your AI-assisted side hustle? Are you wondering how you can see these lucrative side hustles in action? Well, let us go over a few stories about individuals who used AI to build and scale their side hustles.

Jaden's Story

Jaden had always been passionate about writing, but her full-time job in marketing didn't allow her the creative freedom she craved. After reading about the potential of AI in content creation, she decided to explore the world of side hustles. Using AI-generated content, Jaden began a blog focused on affordable travel tips.

At the start, she found a niche with relatively low competition. AI tools helped her generate informative blog posts quickly. As her content quality improved, readership grew steadily. Jaden utilized AI analytics to understand her audience better, refine her blog's focus, and optimize her social media strategy.

Jaden's blog attracted attention, and she started to become a local expert in the field of finding cheaper trips and ways to save money while travelling. She appeared on local television shows, magazines and podcasts. With the increased exposure she soon began to offer AI-driven content services to other bloggers and small businesses. Her side hustle then expanded into a thriving AI-powered content creation agency. With a roster of clients and a team of writers assisted by AI tools, she was generating high-quality content at scale.

AI not only helped Jaden turn her passion for writing into a lucrative side hustle but also enabled her to scale it into a successful business!

Ana's Story

During the pandemic Ana was fortunate enough to keep her job and work from home. However like so many around the world she started to feel bored only staying home. She then started to cook in the spare time she had at home. Her family loved the new recipes she experimented with and she continued to build her confidence as she tried new combinations of foods. Overtime she shared these meals with her extended family and continued to receive tremendous praise.

The idea was given to her by a friend to create a cookbook. Ana initially dismissed the idea as she never considered herself a writer but then she was introduced to Upwork's AI services for writing. She was able to pull together all of her recipes in a book that also incorporated stories of her family and culinary inspirations. She then hired someone who used AI design tools to create a beautiful book cover as well as someone to create a book description and key marketing tips to promote her new project. Ana self-published her book on Amazon and has been able to make passive income to supplement her family's income.

Ethan's Story

Ethan had a background in web development and a deep interest in AI. Seeing the potential to create a unique side hustle, he decided to dive into AI-enhanced web development for e-commerce businesses.

He used AI tools to enhance user experiences, automate customer support through chatbots, and offer personalized product recommendations. These AI-driven features quickly made his clients' websites stand out, leading to high customer satisfaction.

Word of Ethan's expertise spread, and he began to receive more requests than he could handle on his own. To scale his side hustle, he employed a small team of developers and AI specialists. With the help of AI for project management, the team efficiently handled multiple projects simultaneously.

As e-commerce continued to grow, Ethan's AI-backed web development side hustle flourished. He eventually expanded his services to provide AI-enhanced website audits, helping businesses optimize their existing sites. This broadened his reach and made his side hustle even more lucrative.

Through his unique blend of web development skills and AI proficiency, Ethan transformed a side hustle into a thriving business that catered to the ever-growing e-commerce market.

Whatever you wish to do, AI will make it easier—take it from Jaden, Ana and Ethan!

Then, there is Bryant. Do you remember him from Chapter 4? Bryant had turned his investment business around with the help of AI: this is a whole realm of study in itself! How can you use AI to beat the stock market? Moreover, how has AI fared in the stock market so far? These questions and more will be answered in the next chapter on how to use AI for investing. Stay tuned!

Chapter 7: How to Use AI for Investing

Fortunes have been built on the stock market and yet others have been lost there! Investing is a tricky field that requires a combination of quantitative expertise and qualitative "luck." In investing, the ambiguity of arbitrage—which is the part of investing that allows you to make money based off disagreements about the values of things—is one reason for the prevalence of financial planners and professional investors today: these people claim to have the expertise to manage your money. You don't have that expertise, they say, and, so, you pay them! But, how do these financial planners and professional investors do compared to—for example—AI for the purposes of investing?

In this chapter, we will look at how AI has been used for investments, what kind of AI tools are most popular and how they are used, and what the risks are to using AI for investing. If you are a seasoned investor or just getting started, let AI be your financial advisor and it, with the proper precautions, can be your key to an impressive fortune!

How Has AI Done in Investing?

Before I answer the question of how successful AI has been in investing, let us review how financial planners and professional investors do on the stock market. It is an open secret, at least to me, that financial planners and professional investors are not exactly worth the occasionally high fees they charge for their services! A study by Delta Wealth Advisors showed that 80-90% of financial planning firms shut down in the first three years of business (Delta Wealth Advisors, 2022). Mark J. Perry (2018), writing for AEI, concurs that 95% of financial advisors fail to beat the market! So, how well does AI do? Can AI succeed where these financial advisors and professional investors have failed?

So far, it is looking like it can! A report at AnalystAnswers showed that three AI-enhanced exchange traded funds (ETFs) beat the S&P500 by 6% (Analyst Answers, 2023). So, not only did AI manage to beat the market—unlike 95% of financial planners and professional investors—but it did so by 6%!

Now, I'm sure you want to know how you can utilize AI to up your investing game! I turn to the apps you can use now.

AI Investment Tools

There is already a plethora of AI tools to select from for the personal investor, while larger players often integrate AI into their in-house software. An analyst at The Second Angle provides a list of eight tools that I expand on below (The Second Angle, 2023):

- **EquBot.** EquBot's platform utilizes machine learning techniques, knowledge graphs, and IBM's Watson natural language processor. This AI platform, in collaboration with IBM Watson, is specifically designed to assist global investment professionals in delivering enhanced results through portfolios-as-a-service (PaaS). EquBot's features simplify and expedite data analysis, offering on-demand AI portfolios, indexes, and signals. It continuously scans millions of news articles, social media posts, and financial statements daily to generate accurate forecasts.

- **Acorns.** Acorns has gained popularity among the new generation of savings apps due to its straightforwardness. Once set up, users can largely set it and forget it! By linking a debit or credit card to your account, Acorns rounds up your purchases to the nearest dollar and invests the spare change in a variety of ETF portfolios.

- **Round.** Investment apps are increasingly integrating robo-advisors into their services. Round generates user portfolios through an automated questionnaire and collaborates with fund managers like Guggenheim Partners, Doubleline, and Gabelli, by providing private investors access to institutional-grade investments. Round charges a fixed 0.5 percent management fee and exempts this fee in cases of poor returns. Round also employs AI to identify correlations between securities and market expectations, while using machine learning to automate the buying and selling of securities. This app offers end-to-end AI and robotic process automation services from inception to the final product.

- **Wealthfront.** Wealthfront stands as one of the largest independent robo-advisors. It offers its services for a nominal fee whether your funds are in a taxable account or an IRA. Wealthfront constructs portfolios from a vast selection of ETFs, taking into consideration your desired risk level and investment timeline. The platform automatically allocates new deposits to keep your account balanced and aligned with your financial objectives.

- **Fidelity Investments.** Fidelity Investments provides an integrated financial experience, offering various accounts such as investing, checking, IRA, business retirement plans like SEP IRAs, bill payment, savings, robo-advisory services, and even credit cards. You can manage all your financial accounts in one place, enjoying a comprehensive and customer-focused experience.

- **Ellevest.** Ellevest is not only a top robo-advisor but also a leading app for socially responsible investing. Its mission is to empower female investors in making informed investment choices. Ellevest tailors financial portfolios and programs to consider the unique circumstances of women, including their potentially lower lifetime earnings.

- **Blackbox Stocks.** Blackbox Stocks harnesses AI-powered technology known as "The Box" to identify and alert traders to real-time opportunities. The app scans the market for deep-pool activities, which are private exchanges of securities that are hidden to public investors, and provides access to a private chat room for sharing alerts and insights. The trading system includes a pre-market scanner that identifies the most active stocks and displays their volatility.

- **Magnifi.** Harnessing advanced artificial intelligence and generative AI capabilities, Magnifi empowers users to make informed investment decisions. Its AI-driven algorithms provide tailored investment advice, taking into account individual financial goals, risk tolerance, and investment preferences. By leveraging real-time data analysis and market trend monitoring, Magnifi equips investors with the tools to optimize their portfolios, leading to more effective and data-driven investment strategies.

- **WealthSimple.** WealthSimple is a prominent robo-advisor that leverages artificial intelligence to assist investors in managing their portfolios. It constructs diversified portfolios using a combination of low-cost ETFs tailored to the individual's risk tolerance and financial goals. WealthSimple's AI continuously monitors market conditions and automatically rebalances portfolios to optimize returns.

- **Betterment.** Betterment is another robo-advisor known for its advanced AI technology. It offers a range of automated portfolio options that adapt to users' goals and risk preferences. Betterment's AI-driven algorithms work in real-time to manage investments and ensure the portfolio stays aligned with the investor's objectives.

- **M1 Finance.** M1 Finance combines automated investing with customizable portfolio options. It employs AI to allocate funds efficiently based on an investor's preferences. This platform allows users to create and manage their portfolios with the help of dynamic, automated investment strategies.

- **Ally Invest Managed Portfolios.** Ally Invest's Managed Portfolios is a robo-advisor service that employs AI-driven algorithms to create and maintain diversified portfolios for users. It tailors investment strategies to individual risk profiles and objectives while providing real-time monitoring and rebalancing for optimized performance.

- **SigFig.** SigFig is a financial platform that utilizes artificial intelligence to offer personalized investment advice and portfolio management. It provides users with insights into their portfolios, tracks performance, and recommends adjustments to help users achieve their financial goals.

- **WiseBanyan.** WiseBanyan is a robo-advisor that uses AI to provide users with a simple, automated, and cost-effective way to invest. It creates personalized portfolios and automatically rebalances them as needed, based on each individual's financial situation and goals.

- **Motif.** Motif is an investment platform that integrates AI for thematic investing. It enables users to build portfolios around specific themes or investment strategies. The AI technology helps users identify trends and opportunities in line with their chosen motifs.

How AI Tools Are Used for Investing

Consider one of the biggest pitfalls of human investing: loss aversion. Individuals miss out on long term earnings because they worry about short-term losses. It is human nature to sell your holdings early because it is disheartening to see your money disappear when there is a momentary downturn—but not for AI: AI does not feel disheartened—at least not yet! Anyways, to be successful at anything, you need to know the ins-and-outs of the process that you are involved in; that is the totality of what I will say in terms of AI and investing because I am not a financial advisor. Loss aversion is only one component of how AI tools work for the purposes of investing. Let us review the ways in which AI is employed in this field:

Algorithmic trading. Algorithmic trading represents the most direct utilization of AI in investment. Traders employ AI algorithms to swiftly analyze extensive datasets and execute trades based on market trends and patterns. Computers can analyze data much faster than humans, giving them an edge in high-frequency trading. Moreover, AI algorithms are not influenced by human biases, such as the aforementioned loss aversion, anchoring, and framing. Algorithmic trading often concentrates on exploiting price discrepancies like the bid-ask spread, with gains sometimes being marginal, making it effective mainly in high-volume trading. However, it is important to note that no trading strategy is infallible, as market conditions and trader responses to new information can change rapidly.

Sentiment analysis. AI is employed for sentiment analysis in investing, as I discussed in terms of marketing in the last chapter. Market movements are influenced by various factors, including macroeconomic data, earnings reports, geopolitical issues, interest rates, and market sentiment. Sentiment is a challenging element to quantify, but it often has a greater impact on stock markets than any other data. AI programs assist traders in evaluating market sentiment by gathering news articles, social media posts, and other online content to gauge sentiment and predict market movements. Sentiment can significantly affect entire sectors, driving surges in industries like electric vehicles, cannabis, cryptocurrency, and now, AI stocks.

Portfolio optimization. Portfolio management is a fundamental concept in investing, with money managers striving to strike a balance between diversification, risk, income, and growth. AI can aid fund managers in optimizing portfolios to achieve these objectives and prioritize them as needed. Additionally, there is potential for the use of generative AI technologies like ChatGPT in portfolio management, as it can be effective as a co-pilot in portfolio construction. AI can be particularly beneficial for retail investors who may lack experience in managing their investments, though AI investing bots can also offer insights to money managers on how to enhance portfolio balance.

Risk management. AI plays a role in risk management by analyzing historical market data, volatility, and correlations that can impact returns. Machine learning techniques are applied to enhance efficiency and reduce costs in risk management. In some cases, AI can replace human labor, as it can rapidly analyze extensive datasets with minimal human intervention. AI models potentially have superior forecasting accuracy compared to traditional regression models and can capture nonlinear relationships between risk factors and other variables.

Personalized investment advice. With innovations like ChatGPT and generative AI, AI programs are now capable of delivering personalized investment advice. For instance, Magnifi employs ChatGPT and other AI tools to provide real-time investment advice. It functions as an AI-powered trading platform with a chatbot interface. While Magnifi is relatively new, it is likely that more AI-based investing platforms will emerge as investors seek to leverage this new technology. Established trading platforms like Robinhood may also integrate these AI trading tools in the near future.

Risks of AI Trading

Is it really that simple? Should I really let the machine manage my money for me?

Remember back to using AI for your studies, career, or side hustle. Let us say: you are an artist using AI for the purposes of graphic design and content creation. Will you succeed in graphic design and content creation without personalizing your AI output? Probably not. Will you succeed in investment using AI without personalizing your money-making approach? It is harder to say but, not being a financial advisor, I would go on a limb and state that there are possibly several factors and considerations that go beyond the capabilities of AI alone: personalizing your investment strategy entails accounting for your risk tolerance, financial objectives, and even your timeline for investment. Important decisions like this are best understood and managed by you, the investor, with AI serving as a powerful assistant.

Moreover, while AI can excel at data analysis and identifying patterns, it does not fully account for external factors such as economic events, geopolitical shifts, or individual circumstances that can impact investment decisions. This is not yet all! Consider these other risks to investing with AI:

- **Algorithmic Bias.** Like there are biases for human investors, there are biases for AI. AI algorithms can inherit biases present in the data used for training. This can lead to discriminatory outcomes or reinforce existing market biases. In investing, this can result in unequal opportunities for different demographic groups and market inefficiencies.

- **Overreliance on Technology.** If we think about the long-term effects of AI in investing, investors may become overly reliant on AI tools and neglect their own critical thinking and decision-making skills. In times of unforeseen events or rapid market shifts, an overreliance on AI recommendations could lead to suboptimal investment choices.

- **Data Security.** AI investing platforms require access to a significant amount of financial and personal data. Protecting this sensitive information from cyber threats and breaches is a major concern. Unauthorized access to investor data can lead to identity theft and financial loss.

- **Regulatory Challenges.** The use of AI in investing is subject to regulatory oversight. Compliance with existing and evolving regulations can be complex and costly. Violations can lead to legal issues and financial penalties.

- **Lack of Transparency.** AI-driven investment decisions can often lack transparency. Investors might not fully understand how the AI system arrived at a particular recommendation, making it difficult to assess the validity of the advice.

- **Market Manipulation.** There is a risk that AI algorithms can be manipulated or gamed by unscrupulous actors to influence stock prices or trading strategies, potentially leading to market instability.

- **High-Frequency Trading Risks.** AI-driven high-frequency trading can result in rapid and extreme market fluctuations, contributing to market volatility. This can create opportunities for some but pose risks for others.

- **Inadequate Training Data.** The quality and representativeness of the data used to train AI models are critical. If training data is incomplete, outdated, or skewed, AI models may not accurately predict market trends or risks.

- **Black Swan Events.** AI models are typically trained on historical data, which may not account for rare, unforeseen events often referred to as "black swan" events. These events can have a profound impact on financial markets, and AI systems may struggle to adapt.

- **Unpredictable Behavior.** The complexity of AI algorithms can make them challenging to predict. They may behave unpredictably in certain situations, making it difficult for investors to anticipate their responses to market changes.

So, in summary, and not being a financial advisor, I could only speculate that financial success is not only predicated on AI's capacity for data-driven insights. Rather, it could be that financial success hinges on your ability to adapt to dynamic markets, respond to unforeseen challenges, and make informed choices based on your own financial roadmap. AI may provide the instrument, so to speak, but the orchestration of your financial future remains in your hands!

AI's influence in the investment world is undeniable. It seems that whatever influence AI does not yet have in the realm of making money is due to the fact that some players are only catching up to it. Yet, can AI help us in other facets of our life, besides getting better grades, improving our careers, creating a side hustle, and investing? Well, what else is there, exactly? A lot of things! How about our social life? AI's influence in our communication and socialization is paramount, or yet to be. Join me as I discuss AI's increasing prevalence in the social sphere, including in dating apps, in the next chapter. You don't want to miss this!

Chapter 8: How to Use AI to Improve Your Social Life

Imagine this: you have incorporated AI into your studies, career, side hustle, and investments. In a word, you are flourishing! Yet, I often hear about financially successful people feeling lonely. Obviously, life is nothing special without the people in it. So, can AI bring you social rewards in addition to financial ones? I foreshadowed in previous chapters that it can: your entire life can be transformed with AI, including from the people you meet, date, or even marry.

Take it from Jonathan: he met his wife Lola on Tinder, and their meeting was facilitated by the AI learning algorithm that Tinder uses to display matches. Jonathan swiped left and he swiped right enough for the Tinder algorithm to build a profile around Jonathan's preference for a partner. Lola was displayed. Jonathan swiped right; the rest is history.

I began this book talking about the risks of AI. To summarize what I stated earlier, the risks of AI to human autonomy are low unless we give AI the keys to our genetic destiny; that is, we let AI choose for us the people with whom we reproduce. That is unlikely to happen with current apps like Tinder because no one is forcing people to use Tinder or date the people they meet on Tinder. Then, there are less 'existential' risks related to AI, which I also talked about in Chapter 1: does the use of AI deaden the interpersonal nature of our interactions? In general, I see the potential for AI to both widen and flatten human relationships. What do I mean by this?

Consider that Jonathan would have never met Lola without the Tinder AI algorithm: he was exposed to a broader net of people to meet than he could have otherwise had without AI. So, the net was wider. At the same time, Jonathan had the potential to meet not only Lola but Lisa, Pamela, Angela, Rene, and whoever else! Potentially, our relationships facilitated with AI are flatter than they otherwise would have been. If you were a butter-churner at the turn of the twentieth century, your village boyfriend was your world. That is a deep relationship! Today, there is your village boyfriend and a thousand other potential partners. There is always somebody else around the corner, thanks to AI.

Expressing concerns about the trajectory of technology often leads to over-thinking. As I discussed in the case of e-learning in schools, AI is here to stay; including in terms of guiding our social interactions. We ought to make the best of it and use it to our advantage rather than wringing our hands about what could have been if not for this AI revolution! So, with that in mind, let us review how AI has increased our social networks and exposed us to new people we otherwise would not have met thanks to this revolutionary technology.

The Use of AI in Social Networks

You either have a Facebook account or know someone who does! This ever-present social network platform was among the first to integrate AI into its processes of friend recommendation and content curation.

When you log into Facebook, the platform employs AI algorithms to analyze your past interactions, such as the posts you've liked, shared, or commented on, and your connections with other users. Based on this data, the AI system tailors your news feed to display content that is more likely to engage and interest you. Likewise, the friend recommendation system uses AI algorithms to analyze a myriad of data points, including mutual friends, shared interests, common groups, and interactions. This in-depth analysis helps Facebook suggest individuals whom you might know or want to connect with, making the process of expanding your social network more efficient and relevant.

Beyond personalized content, AI also plays a crucial role in enhancing user safety on Facebook. The platform employs AI-powered content moderation tools to identify and remove harmful content, such as hate speech, graphic violence, and misinformation. These algorithms can process and review vast amounts of content quickly, thereby helping to maintain a safe and respectful online environment. When combined with human moderators, these AI systems help in mitigating the spread of harmful or inappropriate content. As you may know from my chapters on marketing, Facebook ads employ AI algorithms to target likely buyers.

In recent years, Facebook has expanded its AI applications to be more accessible. AI-driven features like automatic alt text for images assist users with visual impairments by providing descriptions of images in their news feeds, thereby making the platform more inclusive. In general, AI has transformed global communication by facilitating translation through services like Google Translate, DeepL, and Microsoft Translation. The ability to talk to people across the world has never been easier. The net is wider; I suppose it is on us whether those relationships will be flat!

Elle's Story

Let us now answer the question of how you can improve your social life with AI through Elle, a young professional who moved to a new city for her dream job. She found herself in an unfamiliar environment, far away from her friends and family. While her work was fulfilling, she longed for meaningful social connections and wanted to build a local network of friends.

Enter Instagram: a leading photo and video-sharing social network which has harnessed the power of AI to create a personalized and engaging user experience. When you open the Instagram app, you are immediately greeted by a feed filled with photos and videos. Behind the scenes, AI algorithms are hard at work to ensure that the content you see is tailored to your interests.

Elle made use of Instagram to expand her social network in the following ways:

Connecting with Local Communities. Elle recognized that Instagram could be a powerful tool for discovering local events, groups, and communities. She started following local businesses, event organizers, and community pages related to her hobbies and interests. By doing so, she received regular updates on events, meetups, and gatherings happening in her city.

Exploring Hashtags. Instagram's hashtag system allowed Elle to search for local events and activities. She began using hashtags related to her city and interests, such as #LocalFoodie, #YogaInCityPark, and #ArtGalleryOpenings. This strategy helped her discover like-minded individuals and events where she could engage with people who shared her passions.

Engaging with Local Influencers. Elle also followed local influencers who frequently shared their experiences exploring the city. These influencers often posted about their favorite places to eat, cultural events, and hidden gems in the city. Elle not only found valuable recommendations but also started engaging in the comments sections of these posts, thereby connecting with fellow enthusiasts.

So, how did it go for Elle? By actively using Instagram as a social networking tool, Elle successfully improved her social life. She attended various events, met new friends, and deepened her connection with her new city. Her Instagram journey transformed from a passive scrolling experience into an active tool for building meaningful social connections. By leveraging the platform's features, engaging with local communities, and connecting with like-minded individuals, she not only expanded her social network but also made her new city feel like home!

Marcel's Story

Elle is only one example of someone who improved her social network using Instagram. Let us discuss another Instagram user, Marcel.

Marcel is a young man with disabilities that affect his speech and motor skills. Living with disabilities presented Marcel with challenges in traditional communication. His speech impediment and limited motor skills made it difficult for him to express himself verbally and engage in face-to-face conversations. Feeling isolated, he sought alternative ways to connect with others and discovered the potential of AI on Instagram.

How did Marcel make use of AI to expand his social network? He did the following:

Voice-to-Text Technology. Instagram's integration of voice-to-text technology became a game-changer for Marcel. Instead of struggling to type out messages, he could use his voice to compose captions, comments, and direct messages. This not only made communication more efficient but also allowed him to express himself with greater ease.

Auto-Suggestions and Predictive Text. Marcel took advantage of AI-powered auto-suggestions and predictive text features on Instagram. These capabilities helped him formulate messages faster, reducing the time and effort required for typing. The predictive text feature, which suggests words or phrases as he types, improved the accuracy and speed of his communication.

Engaging through Stories and Captions. Instagram's Stories feature became Marcel's preferred method of sharing his experiences. With AI-enhanced text options, he could create visually appealing and informative stories using voice commands. This feature allowed him to share his daily life, thoughts, and reflections, thereby fostering a deeper connection with his followers.

As a result, by embracing the AI features on Instagram, Marcel transformed his social experience! He not only became an active participant in conversations but also built a supportive community around him. His engaging Stories, powered by AI-driven text options, enabled him to share his unique perspective, experiences, and challenges. Marcel's approach to communication evolved from being a source of frustration to a powerful tool for self-expression and connection.

Using AI For Success on Dating Apps

We are already using AI to make the biggest decision of all: the choice of the person we will spend the rest of our lives with.

A study at Pew Research discovered that 30% of American adults have used a dating app. Meanwhile, 12% of respondents found their long-term partner through a dating app (Perez, 2020). This number is only expected to go up as more people use dating apps and as the AI technology underlying them improves.

Consider OkCupid, a dating website turned app that was founded in 2003. OkCupid utilizes AI to calculate personalized compatibility scores between users. This score is based on a range of factors, including shared interests, values, and responses to specific questions. By leveraging AI, OkCupid strives to enhance the accuracy of these compatibility scores, increasing the likelihood of users finding matches that align with their preferences and values. Moreover, OkCupid's AI continuously refines its understanding of user preferences as individuals engage with the platform. This allows the app to provide dynamic profile recommendations over time. As users interact with profiles and refine their own preferences, the AI system adapts, thereby offering more tailored and relevant matches.

Finally, AI on OkCupid doesn't stop at matchmaking; it extends to optimizing the messaging experience. The platform uses machine learning to analyze successful interactions, learning from user behaviors and preferences. This information is then used to provide users with messaging suggestions that are more likely to initiate engaging conversations.

You may be asking yourself: how do I make use of AI to improve the quality of my matches? In other words, how can I enhance the accuracy and relevance of my potential connections on dating apps? Here are some strategies to make the most of AI for a more personalized and successful dating experience:

- **Complete and Update Your Profile.** Provide detailed information about yourself, your interests, and what you're looking for in a match. The more data you provide, the better AI algorithms can understand your preferences.

- **Answer Compatibility Questions.** Many dating apps, like OkCupid, use compatibility questions to assess your values and preferences. Take the time to answer these questions thoughtfully as they contribute to the AI's understanding of your personality and priorities.

- **Engage with the App.** Regularly use the app to browse profiles, like or dislike matches, and initiate conversations. AI algorithms learn from your interactions, refining their understanding of your preferences over time.

- **Utilize Features Like Smart Photos.** Some apps, such as Tinder, offer features like Smart Photos that use AI to analyze which of your photos receive the most likes. Allow the app to arrange your photos to increase visibility and potentially attract more matches.

- **Review and Adjust Preferences.** Periodically review and adjust your preferences in the app settings. This includes location, age range, and other filters. AI algorithms take these preferences into account when suggesting potential matches.

- **Explore Premium Features.** Consider using premium features offered by dating apps. These features often involve advanced AI algorithms for more refined matching. Features like Boosts or Super Likes may increase your visibility to potential matches.

- **Optimize Your Messaging.** Pay attention to messaging suggestions provided by the app. AI algorithms analyze successful interactions to offer personalized suggestions. Use these prompts to initiate engaging and meaningful conversations. Some dating apps now offer helpful introductory prompts for you if you're feeling shy and don't know how to initiating a conversation. Use all of these helpful tools to your advantage. Everyone else is.

- **Stay Active and Responsive.** Regularly engage with the app and respond promptly to messages. AI algorithms consider user activity and responsiveness when suggesting matches. Being active on the platform increases your chances of receiving relevant recommendations.

- **Provide Feedback.** Some apps allow users to provide feedback on suggested matches. If a match is particularly relevant or not to your liking, share your feedback. This information helps the AI system refine its recommendations.

- **Be Open-Minded.** While specifying preferences is essential, be open-minded to new connections. AI algorithms may introduce you to matches that align with your values even if they don't fit all your specified criteria.

If you want to try another approach to dating using AI, consider having a dating app being your matchmaker. Meaning, allowing AI to choose who you engage with based on the data you share.

Iris. The iris Dating app website explains that it "applies artificial intelligence to understand who you are attracted to and uses that understanding to present you with matches to people who also are attracted to someone like you" (iris 2023).

The company motto is 'where technology meets romance'. This is how the process works: The app creates a profile of new members by putting them through "training" where they are shown faces of "people" of their desired gender. Note that some of the photos are actually stock images and some are even AI-generated. Members are prompted to hit "Pass," "Maybe," or "Like" to these images. The app uses this information to learn a user's physical type, then only offers potential matches with a high data-backed chance of mutual attraction and lower odds of rejection.

AIMM. The AIMM Dating app is also an AI led dating service however it serves as a virtual personal assistant. The personal assistant gives you a thorough personality assessment that is used for its matchmaking process. Throughout the process, your personal assistant will 'coach' or guide you through the introduction and conversational process until you're ready to step out on your own.

And if you are really apprehensive to put yourself out there in the dating world and you would feel better having an opportunity to practice your social and flirting skills, there are AI apps available to help. Dating app startups **Blush and Romantic.ai** will provide a service that can allow you to practice your conversational skills with an AI partner (a bot) in a virtual romantic setting.

So, how do these sound to you? Willing to give any of these a try? While these AI dating app services may not seem ideal to everyone, just think, at one point in time, online dating was once a farfetched idea too.

Of course, the best way to attract a mate—online or off—is by being the best version of yourself! This includes, in large part, taking care of your health. In the next chapter, I talk about the role AI can play in your health. From work-life balance to sleep, fitness, and nutrition, AI can be your companion in making your dreams about your body a reality. If you want to know how AI can improve your health, read on!

Chapter 9: How to Use AI to Improve Your Health

It is reductive to state that your life is only as good as your health, but I'll state it anyway! Anyone who has been sick for a prolonged period of time or observed sickness in a family member knows this to be true: we often don't appreciate good health until we get sick. We don't realize how comparatively easy life is until life gets a lot less easy because of sickness.

The best way to avoid sickness is to prevent it for as long as possible! This is done, as all available evidence suggests, through exercise, healthy eating, and a sound mind (perhaps garnered through meditation). As Thales, the Ancient Greek philosopher puts it, "A sound mind is a sound body" (Bailey, 2014).

Together in *The AI Success Route*, you and I have reviewed AI in your studies, careers, side hustles, investments, and social lives. Now, I turn to your health: perhaps your greatest gift of all!

How AI is Used in Healthcare

There are a plethora of AI-assisted apps designed to help you optimize your health—perhaps the largest list of any category of apps in this book. But, before I get to the ways you can use AI to better your health, let us review how AI is currently used in healthcare and the potential for future applications of AI in healthcare.

Clinical Documentation. Currently, ChatGPT powers chatbots that are utilized for tasks such as assisting patients in evaluating symptoms, scheduling appointments, and supporting outpatient monitoring. An example of this is Nuance's Dragon Ambient eXperience, an AI which records and transcribes interactions between doctors and patients, thereby producing a comprehensive clinical summary within the electronic health record.

According to Ken Harper, Vice President and General Manager of Healthcare Virtual Assistants and Ambient Clinical Intelligence at Nuance, the integration of AI in administrative tasks allows physicians more time for direct patient care (Laviola, 2023). By alleviating a portion of the cognitive burden and fatigue, this AI not only enhances the efficiency of healthcare professionals but also contributes to improved access to care for patients. Harper emphasizes that healthcare organizations have utilized the time saved by AI to accommodate more patients, thereby enhancing accessibility to healthcare services.

Imaging. Envision a scenario where ten million radiologists are scrutinizing a medical scan, in contrast to only a few specialized experts. This is essentially the principle behind how AI is integrated into healthcare imaging. Platforms like Nuance's Precision Imaging Network employ AI algorithms to analyze images and offer insights to radiologists.

According to Mona Flores, Global Head of AI at NVIDIA, AI plays a pervasive role in contemporary imaging practices, potentially aiding in reducing diagnostic errors by identifying anomalies that a human observer might miss (Lavola, 2023). The key advantage of AI lies in its ability to learn from an immense volume of data. An AI tool trained to recognize various manifestations of a disease in imaging studies can swiftly draw conclusions from new studies—without succumbing to fatigue, a challenge for its human counterparts!

Patient Monitoring. The adoption of wearable devices utilizing AI has enabled healthcare providers to expand remote patient monitoring, tracking and analyzing data such as blood pressure, glucose levels, and sleep patterns.

Virtual nursing platforms, exemplified by services from Artisight and Caregility, leverage smart technology to monitor large patient populations. The

AI tool within these platforms is trainable to identify potential issues, deliver automated messages to patients, and notify in-person care teams.

Ryan Cameron, Vice President of Technology and Innovation at Children's Hospital and Medical Center in Nebraska, notes that his organization is actively developing AI-driven systems to automate decision support for healthcare providers (Laviola, 2023). As part of this initiative, Cameron describes a project focused on real-time monitoring of vital signs, wherein the AI tool compares patient data against various sources, employs complex calculations, and provides infusion recommendations for doctors to assess.

Research. In the regular form of drug development, the path from conceptualizing a new therapy to its actual implementation for patient use is a protracted process, often spanning several years. This timeline is influenced by the meticulous phases of research, experimentation, clinical trials, and regulatory approvals that collectively ensure the safety and efficacy of any novel drug.

However, the advent of generative AI tools, exemplified by the NVIDIA BioNeMo Service, is transforming the current paradigm. By harnessing the power of artificial intelligence and accelerated computing, BioNeMo introduces a revolutionary approach to drug discovery. The conventional timelines are compressed as this innovative tool empowers researchers to rapidly generate potential candidate drugs and subject them to rigorous testing within a simulated environment (Laviola, 2023).

The acceleration of the drug discovery process through BioNeMo is particularly noteworthy for its potential impact on addressing rare diseases. The traditional model often faces challenges in efficiently developing therapies for these conditions due to their limited prevalence. By leveraging generative AI, researchers can streamline the cycle of drug development, making it not only faster but also more cost-effective.

Surgery and Robotics. AI-powered robotics have become an integral component in the realm of minimally invasive surgeries, with surgeons relying on advanced technologies such as the da Vinci Surgical System, instituted by Intuitive Surgeries for a substantial number of laparoscopic procedures (Laviola, 2023).

In these instances, achieving perfect stillness during surgery is a formidable challenge for a human operator, given the inherent factors like breathing and heart rate. Herein lies the pivotal role played by the da Vinci system: this sophisticated technology is designed not only to accommodate but also to absorb the natural movements of the surgeon's body, ensuring that every maneuver is executed with unparalleled precision.

The da Vinci Surgical System's AI-driven capabilities address a longstanding challenge in surgery: the inherent limitations of human physiology. By seamlessly integrating with the surgeon's movements and compensating for physiological factors that could introduce variability, this robotic system transcends the constraints of traditional surgical approaches. The result is a level of precision and steadiness that might be unattainable through conventional means.

Genetic Engineering and AI: A New Frontier in Medicine

What if we could genetically engineer people to be free from disease, or be stronger, or have six fingers on each hand? Well, this prospect of genetic engineering, which AI will undoubtedly play a role in, carries ethical considerations, not only for the people undergoing genetic engineering but those that have to compete with them on a market for jobs and partners. Though, this innovation in medicine will probably come about, so it is worth considering the role that AI will play in it!

AI can be synergized with revolutionary gene-editing technologies like CRISPR (Clustered Regularly Interspaced Short Palindromic Repeats). In fact, the synergistic marriage of AI and CRISPR holds great promise in fields such as biotechnology, medicine, and agriculture, despite the aforementioned risks it carries. Here is a closer look at the role of AI in genetic engineering and CRISPR:

Efficient Target Identification. One of the early and crucial steps in genetic engineering is identifying the specific genes to be targeted for modification. AI-driven algorithms can swiftly analyze massive datasets of genetic information, helping scientists pinpoint genes associated with particular traits or conditions. This accelerates the target identification process for CRISPR-based gene editing.

Off-Target Prediction and Minimization. A major concern with CRISPR is the potential for off-target effects where unintended genetic changes occur. AI models can predict these off-target sites, allowing researchers to design CRISPR systems with minimal off-target impact. By reducing off-target errors, AI enhances the precision and safety of gene editing.

Optimized Guide RNA Design. The selection of guide RNAs is critical for guiding CRISPR-Cas9 to the intended gene location. AI algorithms can design highly effective guide RNAs by considering factors like sequence specificity, target gene accessibility, and potential off-target effects. This leads to more accurate and efficient gene editing.

Accelerated Drug Discovery. As I mentioned in terms of drug development, AI-driven platforms analyze genetic data to identify potential drug targets and candidate compounds. By understanding the genetic basis of diseases more comprehensively, researchers using AI can develop treatments and therapies that are tailored to an individual's unique genetic makeup, known as precision medicine.

Agricultural Advancements. AI is helping to engineer crops with improved traits such as higher yield, pest resistance, and drought tolerance. By analyzing genetic data and applying CRISPR techniques, scientists can develop crops that are more resilient, environmentally friendly, and better suited to address global food security challenges.

Data Management and Analysis. Genetic engineering generates vast amounts of data, which AI tools efficiently manage and analyze. This data includes genomic sequences, experimental results, and clinical records. AI algorithms can help identify patterns, correlations, and insights that would be difficult for humans to discern, enabling faster breakthroughs.

Human Genome Interpretation. AI systems are aiding in the interpretation of human genomes, thereby helping to uncover the genetic basis of various diseases. They can identify potential genetic markers for conditions, allowing for early detection and personalized treatment plans.

Automation and Experiment Planning. AI-driven robotics are automating the CRISPR experiment process. These robots can precisely execute the gene-editing steps, thereby freeing scientists from repetitive tasks and ensuring reproducibility. AI can also assist in experiment planning, recommending optimal conditions and protocols.

How You Can Use AI to Better Your Health

As I mentioned at the start of this chapter, the best path to good health is to avoid getting sick in the first place! So, let us hope you are not making your way through the healthcare system—if you are, this system is increasingly powered by AI—but trying to avoid it entirely! Now, let us look at apps that will help you stay healthy and avoid the healthcare system except for your yearly physical—an apple a day may keep the doctor away, and AI will both literally and metaphorically remind you to eat it!

Work-life Balance Tools

Work-life balance tools work to make the tasks you have to complete, especially at work, more efficient. They help you to prioritize the most important duties, emails and outputs in your day upfront. We spend so much of our time sifting through meaningless emails that can overload our brains. In an effort to have a good work-life balance, AI tools can help you sift through the 'noise' in our inboxes and to-do lists and focus on what's most important and avoid bringing undue stress and exhaustion.

Sane-Box. Sane-box is an email management tool that helps you organize your emails and prioritize which messages are most important. This program can save you time and keep you focused on what you need to get done at work and get you out living and enjoying life.

Toggl. Toggl is a time management tracking AI tool. It can help you to determine how much time you're spending on different tasks and activities at work, while studying or spending time online. It can be a very eye-opening experience when you look at how long you spend using up precious time doing mundane activities that aren't necessary. Toggl will analyze your time management history and help you to balance your work and personal life.

Sleep Tools

Pod AI by Eightsleep. Unlock the secrets of sleep, health, and longevity with Pod AI. This remarkable platform offers round-the-clock, AI-driven answers to your inquiries, ensuring that you have a wealth of knowledge at your fingertips whenever you need it. What sets Pod AI apart is its rigorous training on scientific journals and expert insights, making it a reliable source for accurate and up-to-date information. Whether you have questions about sleep patterns, health-related concerns, or strategies for achieving longevity, Pod AI provides valuable insights that can empower you to make informed decisions about your well-being, helping you lead a healthier and more fulfilling life.

The FRENZ Brainband. Meet the FRENZ Brainband by Earable, a remarkable leap forward in sleep technology. This AI-infused headband adapts to your individual sleep patterns, offering personalized suggestions to enhance your sleep quality. Packed with precision technology, it continuously processes real-time data, providing customized stimuli that promote deep, restful sleep. Beyond improving sleep, it leverages your brainwaves to enhance focus and relaxation by curating audio content tailored specifically for you.

Sleep Number 360 Smart Bed Series. Take a look at the Sleep Number 360 smart bed series, a pioneering innovation designed to not just improve your sleep but revolutionize it. Powered by SleepIQ technology, this bed adapts to your every move, ensuring that each night's sleep experience is exquisitely tailored to you through the power of artificial intelligence. The Sleep Number 360 distinguishes itself with its remarkable AI-driven design, capable of sensing your movements and making automatic adjustments in firmness, comfort, and support to provide you with the coziest night's sleep possible. Moreover, this bed offers customizable comfort on each side, catering to different sleep preferences. In some models, AI even manages temperature regulation during sleep.

Muse S (Gen 2). The Muse S (Gen 2) is a groundbreaking device designed to significantly enhance your sleep quality. This AI-powered gadget delivers responsive sleep experiences, assisting you in transitioning into deep, restful slumber by calming your active mind. It incorporates innovative smart-fade technology to prepare your brain for sleep and gently guide you back to slumber-land if you awaken during the night.

Wyze Smart Floor Lamp. Experience a new level of lighting with the Wyze Smart Floor Lamp. This AI-powered lamp takes personalization to the next level by learning and adapting to your preferred lighting settings for a truly individualized experience. The Wyze Smart Floor Lamp boasts an innovative design, featuring 15 sets of individual condenser lenses. These lenses precisely focus light at a 23-degree angle, enhancing color vibrancy, readability, and minimizing disruptions to those around you. This is perfect for creating a serene bedtime atmosphere that won't disturb your partner's sleep.

The Happy Ring. The Happy Ring is a fusion of style and advanced technology, an AI-powered wearable that goes beyond the ordinary. It is designed to track and interpret your daily habits, aiming to provide deeper insights into your overall well-being. Distinguished by its advanced biometric platform, the Happy Ring captures clinical-grade data from your daily life and employs AI to decipher patterns. These insights can drive meaningful lifestyle changes, potentially enhancing your sleep quality and other facets of your health.

Ambi Climate Mini. The Ambi Climate Mini introduces a new dimension to climate control with the power of AI. This intelligent AC and heat pump controller optimizes your bedroom environment to ensure perfect sleep every time. Leveraging AI, the Ambi Climate Mini responds to fluctuations in weather, humidity, and temperature to maintain your ideal sleep conditions. Its sleek design seamlessly integrates into any room, offering versatile installation options for your smart home ecosystem.

Josh.ai. Transform your living space with the Josh.ai smart home system, a comprehensive solution designed to understand and seamlessly execute your commands. This AI-driven system brings advanced technology to your fingertips, ensuring a smooth and effortless control of your smart home devices. Josh.ai employs cutting-edge voice technology and an intuitive user interface to deliver an unparalleled home automation experience. The system's advanced AI learns your preferences and habits over time, creating a unique, personalized experience for each user. Whether you prefer mobile, desktop, or hands-free microphones, Josh.ai ensures a consistent, user-friendly experience across devices.

Fitness and Nutrition

BurnBacon. Embark on a holistic health journey with BurnBacon, your personalized fitness coach and AI chef, Mia. Discover healthy recipes tailored to your taste, and elevate your workouts with AI coach Ben. From nutritious meals to expert-guided workouts, BurnBacon caters to your unique health goals with AI expertise.

GlowAI. Experience the future of skincare with GlowAI, your personalized skincare routine generator. Crafted based on your budget, skin type, and concerns, GlowAI ensures that your skincare regimen aligns perfectly with your unique needs. With AI-powered insights and continual adaptation, this app is like having a personal skincare expert at your fingertips, making radiant, healthy skin more attainable than ever.

GymGenie. Elevate your fitness journey with GymGenie, where AI meets personalization. GymGenie crafts tailor-made workout routines with a staggering count of 100,000 generated at the time of this writing (GymGenie, n.d.). But, that's not all!—supercharge your fitness odyssey with AI-driven meal plans finely tuned to your health goals. Effortlessly log your meals and snacks, receiving instant analyses of calories, protein, carbohydrates, and fats.

Kayyo. Whether you're a martial arts beginner or a seasoned competitor, Kayyo is your guide to improvement. Access beginner-friendly tutorials and world-class training programs, continually expanding content to help you enhance your martial arts skills. Kayyo's AI-driven feedback and performance tracking take your training to the next level.

MealMind. Addressing the challenge of maintaining a nutritious diet during hectic workweeks, MealMind, an AI-powered meal-planning tool, helps create personalized meal plans, interactive shopping lists, and wellness-focused recipes. Mealmind promotes mindful eating, trying new recipes, simplifying grocery shopping, and offers real-time nutritional insights to support your health and well-being.

Neutrino. Neutrino is an application focused on providing users with nutrition-related insights and data. It has emerged as a leading platform for offering AI-driven fitness services. Neutrino employs a combination of mathematical models and natural language processing (NLP) to deploy predictive analytics for creating customized data summaries.
This startup, established in Israel in 2011, caters to pregnant women, particularly offering personalized nutritional guidance to meet their specific dietary needs. In a noteworthy collaboration, Neutrino has harnessed the NLP capabilities of IBM to deliver

round-the-clock support and dietary recommendations.

FitnessAI. FitnessAI is an innovative fitness app that tailors workout plans to the unique needs of each user. Initially designed as gym-exclusive software, it has since been updated to cater to the growing demand for at-home fitness solutions. What sets FitnessAI apart is its bold claim to outperform any human fitness trainer due to its algorithm's training on a vast dataset of over 5.9 million workouts. Over a span of three years, it meticulously analyzed more than 10 million sets, weights, and repetitions from approximately 30,000 experienced gym enthusiasts and weightlifters (FitnessAI, n.d.).

Freeletics. Freeletics may not claim to surpass the expertise of a human fitness trainer, but it holds a prominent position as a widely recognized fitness app across Europe. It empowers users to maintain an active lifestyle and engage in fitness challenges from anywhere, all while benefiting from AI-driven fitness recommendations. As stated by its CEO, "85% of our users find AI-generated workouts to be exceptional" (ThinkLL, 2022).

Freeletics' coaching algorithm provides users with nutrition and exercise guidance grounded in scientific research, their personal input, and individual preferences. Moreover, it features a community platform where users can share their achievements, engage in discussions, and serve as sources of inspiration for one another.

Suggestic. This app employs a machine learning algorithm to gather health data from individuals by utilizing tracking devices and food logging, enabling it to offer personalized food recommendations. Its AI-powered bot is available to respond to user inquiries at any time. Furthermore, its augmented reality functionality suggests menu items when users are seated at a restaurant and point their app towards the menu list.

Vi Trainer. Utilizing AI, this virtual fitness coach assists users in reaching their fitness goals by providing motivation to run more frequently. Immediately upon installing the application, Vi Trainer delivers a highly customized training plan tailored to your age, gender, current physical condition, and desired objectives. The Vi fitness AI app is actively engaged in initiating enjoyable and dynamic real-time training to personalize user experiences according to their preferences. Additionally, its unique bio-sensing headphones set it apart from other similar alternatives. It offers exercise routines that can be completed both indoors and outdoors.

Calorie Mama. This app employs image classification and AI-driven technology to accurately identify various foods. When presented with an image, Calorie Mama can calculate the calorie content of the depicted dish. Its food AI is trained to recognize and categorize global cuisines, rendering it the top choice for food identification.

Lark. Lark is a contemporary fitness application designed for conversational interaction with users, thereby functioning as both a weight management and human fitness training coach. Its remarkable AI chatbot offers engaging health recommendations, catering to both iOS and Android users. It leverages data from renowned global nutrition experts and user device information to monitor lifestyle decisions, physical activities, and daily routines. Lark inquires about dietary preferences, enabling it to propose personalized meal plans, health insights, sleep patterns, and exercise regimens.

Meditation and Mental Health Support

Breathhh. Known as the "Workplace Wellbeing Companion," Breathhh is a Chrome extension monitoring browser interactions to suggest mental health exercises at opportune moments, alleviating stress and promoting activity. Breathhh's AI-driven monitoring of web activity makes it smarter in predicting suitable times for mental health focus compared to traditional smartwatches. The extension effectively recommends and illustrates wellness activities.

Huberman AI. Embark on a scientific exploration with Huberman AI, the virtual guide to The

Huberman Lab's wisdom. Pose your science or health-related queries and receive AI-backed responses derived from the wealth of knowledge in Huberman Lab episodes. Dive into specific topics or protocols with ease, and obtain timestamped YouTube links for a seamless learning experience.

Flourish. Nurture your mental health with Flourish, an AI-powered self-therapy app featuring Fleur, your AI therapist. Engage in evidence-based advice, goal setting, cognitive-behavioral therapy, and reflective journaling, providing personalized strategies for a resilient mental life.

Sage. Meet Sage, your AI-powered personal health assistant, ready to guide you 24/7. Pose questions and receive customized suggestions on diet, exercise, stress management, and sleep through your favorite messenger. Sage simplifies healthy eating with personalized meal ideas and shopping lists, providing comprehensive advice for a balanced lifestyle.

Insightful. Transform your life with Insightful, an AI-powered coaching tool tailored to individuals. Accessible anytime, anywhere, and covering various topics like career, relationships, and life, Insightful harnesses AI to empower users with personalized guidance.

Reflectr. Declutter your mind with Reflectr, an AI-powered notebook for reflection, growth, and productivity. Enjoy a personal and private digital space for your thoughts, organized and summarized by AI. Reflectr offers a free version with ads or a premium plan for an ad-free experience.

MindGuide. Empower your mental wellness journey with MindGuide, an AI-powered mental health counseling tool that leverages the latest advancements in AI to provide personalized guidance and advice. By harnessing the power of cutting-edge technology, MindGuide offers a holistic approach to mental well-being, enabling users to gain valuable insights, develop effective coping strategies, and navigate life's challenges with confidence and resilience.

Headspace. Headspace, a widely recognized application, takes users through numerous meditations and focus music sessions. This app proves beneficial for designated "focus time" during weekdays for deep work and is invaluable for concentration and relaxation. Headspace's AI-driven customization of meditation sessions can establish a daily meditation habit, significantly enhancing stress management and overall well-being.

Welltory. For real-time stress level feedback and effective work stress management, Welltory, a scientifically-backed app, employs AI to analyze heart rate variability and stress levels. Welltory provides insights into the body's response to work-related situations, thereby contributing significantly to optimizing work routines for better mental health.

Habit Forming and Success Change

Fingerprint for Success. Unlock your potential with Fingerprint for Success, which offers AI-curated online coaching. Set your goals, and their AI magic crafts the perfect coaching plan based on your unique traits and aspirations. Dive into scientific insights about your talents and blind spots, and pair them with wellbeing coaching for a transformative journey.

Mynd. Mynd, a revolutionary journaling app, leverages AI to identify patterns and insights from your entries. Gain immediate insights into your thoughts and experiences as Mynd connects the dots between repeated keywords, themes, and emotions, offering a unique perspective on your thought patterns.

AI Coach Bud. Stay motivated and achieve your goals with AI Coach Bud, a mobile app that goes beyond traditional coaching by offering personalized guidance through daily reminders, progress checks, actionable insights, and a unique accountability buddy system, thereby ensuring you're consistently on track to meet your objectives.

Quazilla by Squad. Quazilla, an AI-powered personal coaching tool, assists users in setting and achieving personalized goals. Driven by ChatGPT, it offers emotional support and guidance at any time, helping users cultivate positive habits and achieve their aspirations. Whether your questions are related to personal growth, career development, or relationship management, Quazilla's AI-driven guidance can be a valuable resource for tailored advice and motivation in your pursuit of success and well-being.

Insumo. Insumo is a mobile application that employs AI to support individuals in making constructive transformations in their lives. This app monitors an individual's advancement and offers customized guidance and coaching tailored to their distinct objectives and obstacles. With Insumo, users can receive actionable insights and motivation, making it easier for them to achieve their personal growth targets.

General Health and Wellbeing

Nuance Dragon Ambient Experience (DAX). Consider DAX as an intelligent assistant tailored for doctors. During patient visits, this innovative tool actively listens and converts conversations into detailed medical notes through advanced technology. Beyond simplifying paperwork, DAX enhances patient care by allowing physicians to maintain eye contact rather than focusing on a keyboard. While clinical scribes have been in use, the fully automated DAX Copilot, interacting with OpenAI's GPT-4 model since September, marks a significant advancement.

Azure AI. Azure AI, a cloud-based service, serves as a swift and reliable information source for both healthcare professionals and patients. Leveraging authoritative data from entities like the US Food and Drug Administration (FDA) and the National Institutes of Health (NIH), this service employs a "text analytics for health" feature to rapidly sift through diverse documents and extract crucial medical information, even in multiple languages if needed. The "AI health insights" feature provides clinicians with a comprehensive view of patient history, simplifies medical reports for patients, and identifies errors in radiology reports. Azure AI is available in both pay-as-you-go and subscription plans.

Hoku. Meet Hoku, your AI health coach syncing seamlessly with your data to provide tailored guidance. This virtual health ally learns your preferences and offers tools to optimize your well-being. Imagine that there is someone who is in your corner delivering recommendations and motivation customized to your unique health profile. From tough love to gentle nudges, Hoku empowers you to generate custom health plans instantly, covering everything from meal plans to exercise routines.

HealthGPT. HealthGPT's mission is to revolutionize health and wellness through accurate, convenient, and free AI-driven tools. Their Prevent tool analyzes your lifestyle, medical history, and genetics to identify potential health risks, while their Diagnose tool offers reliable insights into potential health issues.

Medical Chat. Navigate the complexities of medical specialties with Medical Chat, an advanced AI chatbot for health professionals. Powered by GPT technology, this chatbot delivers precise answers to intricate medical questions, offering immediate information on specialties, patient education, and medications with cited sources.

Mindsum. Ask questions and seek information on mental health topics with Mindsum AI, a conversational tool powered by OpenAI. Benefit from personalized responses and insights derived from custom-trained models. Mindsum AI fosters a supportive environment for users seeking information and guidance on mental health by offering a valuable resource for understanding and addressing a variety of mental wellness topics.

MedGPT. Access information on medicines, treatments, and diagnoses with MedGPT, an AI-powered medication guide offering precise details based on the ChatGPT API. With its simple search feature, MedGPT enables users to input the name of a medication or a specific medical condition and receive comprehensive information, thereby enhancing their knowledge of various healthcare-related topics. Whether you are a healthcare professional or an individual seeking accurate information, MedGPT serves as a valuable tool to provide rapid and reliable insights for informed decisions.

Google Vertex AI Search. Google Vertex AI Search can be envisioned as an exceptionally intelligent search engine designed explicitly for medical professionals. This sophisticated tool swiftly retrieves information from diverse sources such as patient records, notes, and scanned documents. Clinicians can utilize this tool to access information, answer queries, and caption images, extending its capabilities to tasks like billing, clinical trials, and data analysis. The cost structure for Google Vertex AI Search is determined by factors such as data type, features, and the specific model employed, allowing for flexibility in pricing based on usage needs.

Transhumanism and Foreshadowing the Future of AI

Think back to one of the strongest aspects of AI in the healthcare system that I mentioned at the start of the chapter: drug development. Greg Licholai (2023), writing for *Forbes*, illustrates why AI is so effective in this field:

> Traditionally, the discovery process for new medicines has been painstakingly slow, taking up to 26 months before clinical trials even

begin. AI can drastically accelerate this process by predicting the best drug candidates and designing drugs tailored to specific targets. Already, the first drug designed entirely with AI has entered clinical trials in China, and estimates suggest AI could create 50 new therapies over a decade, potentially reducing development costs by billions annually.

One can imagine, in part because it has already happened to some degree, that AI will also be used in surgery and robotics. Undoubtedly, AI can accelerate humanity's entry into what is known as 'transhumanism' by making augmented abilities a reality. Writing for *The Guardian*, Robin McKie (2018) remarks, "In many cases ... technological or medical advances are made to help the injured, sick or elderly but are then adopted by the healthy or young to boost their lifestyle or performance." He quotes Blay Whitby, AI expert at Sussex University: "We are now approaching the time when, for some kinds of track sports such as the 100-meter sprint, athletes who run on carbon-fiber blades will be able to outperform those who run on natural legs" (McKie, 2018). Is it ethical for humans to replace our healthy limbs with computerized ones for the purposes of athletic performance, or to help us live longer?

Kevin Warwick, a cybernetics expert at Coventry University, seems to think it is: "What is wrong with replacing imperfect bits of your body with artificial parts that will allow you to perform better—or which might allow you to live longer?" Warwick admits he is ahead of the curve: "One [device implanted into me] allowed me to experience ultrasonic inputs. It gave me a bat sense, as it were. I also interfaced my nervous system with my computer so that I could control a robot hand and experience what it was touching. I did that when I was in New York, but the hand was in a lab in England" (McKie, 2018).

AI will make our dreams a reality, but you may interpret these dreams to be nightmares! For me, I do not pick a side. I realized early on that AI could benefit me in my work. I saw that it did. Then, AI benefited me in other aspects of life, such as my social life. I took it upon myself to write a book that would outline the benefits about AI while being clear-headed about the risks. If robot hands and implanted chips are nightmarish to you, then so be it! There are many nightmares in this world that are ongoing. Perhaps we have only seen the beginning!

But, it is not like us humans to stop living because of some potential catastrophe on the horizon. That is what separates us from machines: we keep going for the sake of it no matter what the calculation is, and we are perhaps all the more better for it.

Chapter 10: The Future of AI

When it comes to the future of AI it's safe to say that the future is now!

In *The AI Success Route*, I have talked about several ways in which AI is bound to impact your life, and I have discussed how to make use of AI for your academic, business, and social success. There are realms where AI will be used that should be acknowledged with some exploration, and others I cannot even envision! Part of the danger—and fun—in writing about a topic like AI is that there are many unknowns to this revolutionary technology. Your guess is as good as any other in many cases! In this chapter, I venture to make a few guesses based on the emerging discussions happening in technological spaces.

In an article for *Forbes*, Jean-Batiste Hironde (2023), CEO of the mobile app studio MWM, sums up the incredible power of AI which I have discussed in this book:

> Utilizing emerging technologies like AI has broken new ground in providing personalized services to our customers. The ability of AI to analyze vast volumes of data and identify unique patterns has empowered businesses to

predict customer needs with increased accuracy. This predictive power has revolutionized product recommendations and customer service interactions, providing a level of personalization that boosts customer satisfaction, influences purchasing decisions and enhances customer engagement.

With this new power, though, comes concerns, especially about privacy. Hironde (2023) admits, "The data that allows businesses to provide personalized experiences could potentially infringe on personal privacy if not handled correctly. Consequently, consumers are demanding greater transparency about how their data is used and protected." It is not only up to us to act to make sure our privacy is protected with the uptake of AI by patronizing businesses that protect our privacy—it is the responsibility of governments.

There have been the future of AI summits and conferences happening all around the world. A growing number of governments are actively seeking input from their citizens on matters related to AI. You, dear reader—armed with the insight you garnered from this book—can be a strong voice calling for AI to be used responsibly.

The best way to see the future, as much as this is possible, is to look at cutting-edge sections of the greater society. How is AI being used there? Then, when we observe this fact, we can assume this down to our day-to-day lives. As Hironde (2023) puts it, "The reactions of surprise and excitement that many consumers initially express when encountering AI technologies like chat GPT often disappear over time. Like other technologies naturally seeping into our daily lives, it is likely that these convenient AI-enabled services will eventually be taken for granted." In other words AI will become even more common place and incorporated into our daily lives.

In Chapter 3, I described how to use AI to benefit your studies. Now, I'll elaborate on how AI could impact education itself: AI can play a pivotal role in personalized learning. AI-driven platforms can adapt to individual students' learning styles and pace, making education more accessible and effective for everyone. AI-powered tutoring systems and tools for grading and assessment are also emerging, which can aid both students and educators in improving the educational experience. In Chapter 9, I suggested to you how one can use AI to benefit one's mental health. There are now emerging AI technologies that may change mental healthcare practice: chatbots and virtual mental health assistants can provide support to those in need. AI can also assist therapists in treatment planning and tracking patient progress.

In Chapters 3-5, I focused on harnessing the power of AI for your business opportunities in your career and on social media. I implied how, in the financial industry, AI-driven tools help individuals manage their finances more efficiently. Chatbots and robo-advisors are increasingly offering personalized financial advice, automated budgeting, and investment strategies. Additionally, AI is used more and more to detect fraudulent activities, making transactions and financial data more secure.

In Chapter 6, I remarked on how to utilize AI to benefit your social life. AI-powered coaching and self-help apps are evidently on the rise. These platforms can provide personalized recommendations for self-improvement, track progress, and offer guidance in areas such as fitness, nutrition, and personal growth. Users of these platforms increasingly benefit from AI-based, customized plans that align with their goals and preferences.

I'd now like to spend some time exploring two aspects of our lives where AI will regularly play an outsized role: transportation and the environment. Let me say a word on these now.

The future of transportation is always at the forefront of a paradigm shift, and AI is playing a pivotal role in this transformation. AI-driven innovations in mobility encompass a range of advancements, most notably autonomous vehicles and the concept of smart city planning. These developments hold the promise of significantly improving the way we move within and between cities, with the potential to revolutionize safety, efficiency, accessibility, and environmental impact.

One of the most compelling facets of this future is the rise of autonomous vehicles, which I touched on in Chapter 2. These vehicles, equipped with AI algorithms and a multitude of sensors, promise safer roads, reduced traffic congestion, and optimized energy consumption. Their ability to navigate and react to real-time data offers the potential to minimize accidents caused by human error and create a more streamlined, efficient commuting experience. Furthermore, autonomous vehicles can provide newfound accessibility for individuals with disabilities and the elderly, offering greater mobility and independence.

In addition to autonomous vehicles, AI is the cornerstone of smart city planning, where transportation is seamlessly integrated into urban development. Through AI-driven traffic management systems, optimized public transportation, and the promotion of sustainable mobility, smart cities aim to reduce congestion and pollution while enhancing transportation safety. Real-time urban mobility apps empower residents with valuable information on transit options and road conditions, ensuring that they can make informed decisions about their transportation choices. As the fusion of AI, autonomous vehicles, and smart city planning takes shape, we can look forward to a future where transportation becomes safer, more efficient, and environmentally sustainable.

Likewise, AI's role in environmental preservation and sustainability is becoming increasingly significant, because it offers innovative solutions to address the urgent challenges of our changing climate. AI-driven technologies have the potential to revolutionize the way we monitor and manage environmental resources, predict environmental changes, and develop strategies to combat climate change. This impact spans across various sectors, from agriculture and energy to wildlife conservation and waste management.

A key area where AI demonstrates its environmental prowess is in resource management. AI-powered systems can collect and analyze data from various sources to optimize resource allocation. For instance, in agriculture, AI can assess soil conditions, weather patterns, and crop health to recommend precise irrigation and fertilizer application, reducing water and chemical usage. Similarly, in the energy sector, AI can optimize power grid operations and facilitate the integration of renewable energy sources, enhancing energy efficiency and reducing greenhouse gas emissions.

Furthermore, AI's predictive capabilities are instrumental in environmental monitoring. Machine learning models can analyze vast datasets to forecast climate trends, such as extreme weather events and rising sea levels. These predictions enable better disaster preparedness and resource allocation.

Additionally, AI assists in wildlife conservation by tracking endangered species, monitoring their habitats, and helping prevent illegal poaching.

Take another fundamental aspect of human experience: entertainment. AI is not just in the algorithms for Netflix and Spotify that introduce you to new content which I described at the start of this book. Rather, AI is the content itself: music and movies. Let us take a look at how AI is going to shape entertainment in the very near future.

AI Music

Justin Moore and Anish Anchara (2023), writing for technology-focused venture capital firm Andreesen Horowitz, point out that "it's been an eventful year in the world of generative music." What happened in 2023? Well, in April, the music world witnessed the debut of the first viral AI-generated cover, ghostwriter's rendition of "Heart on My Sleeve," which shed light on the potential for AI-generated content to not only exist but also to be of high quality. Shortly thereafter, Google introduced MusicLM, a text-to-music tool that composes songs based on simple prompts, while Paul McCartney employed AI to extract John Lennon's voice for a new Beatles song. Grimes also made waves by offering creators a 50% share of royalties for songs using an AI replica of her voice.

One of the most significant developments was Meta's decision to open source MusicGen: a music generation model capable of transforming text prompts into top-notch musical samples. This action catalyzed the creation of numerous new applications that leverage and expand upon the model, empowering individuals to craft their own music tracks.

There are now several powerful tools that allow you to make music with AI. Among these include Amper Music, Jukedeck, Magenta Studio, AIVA (Artificial Intelligence Visual Artist), and OpenAI Musenet. Moore and Anchara (2023) compare these tools to brand new musical instruments of old, such as synthesizers (emphasis in original): "Similar to how instruments, recorded music, synthesizers, and samplers all supercharged the number of creators and consumers of music when they were introduced, we believe that generative music will help artists make a similar creative leap by blurring the lines between artist, consumer, producer, and performer. By dramatically reducing the friction from idea to creation, AI will allow more people to make music, while also boosting the creative capabilities of *existing* artists and producers."

Indeed, AI only serves to extend and expand the musical space—and to help out artists! Here are some other ways that AI is increasingly involved in music:

Real-time Music Streaming. Thus far, most of the emerging generative streaming products have been in the functional music category: apps like Endel, Brain.fm, and Aimi. They generate never-ending playlists to help you get into a certain mood or headspace, and then adapt based on the time of day and your activity. (However, functional music is starting to converge with traditional music, as powerhouse labels like UMG partner with generative music companies like Endel to create "functional" versions of popular new releases.)

In the Endel app, you can hear how the sound is quite different if you're in "deep work" mode vs. "trying to relax" mode. Endel has also partnered with creatives to produce soundscapes based on their work, like a generative album.

AI Covers. AI-generated covers emerged as one of the pioneering and compelling applications of AI in the music domain. Following the release of "Heart on My Sleeve" in April, AI covers quickly gained immense popularity, amassing over 10 billion views on TikTok under the #aicover label.

A substantial portion of this trend originated within the AI Hub Discord community, which boasted over 500,000 members before its closure in early October due to recurrent copyright violation claims. As discussed further below, the legal concerns associated with AI covers remain unresolved. Consequently, this community has fragmented into more private groups where participants work on training and sharing voice models for specific characters or artists. Many of these efforts employ retrieval-based voice conversion techniques, effectively transforming a clip of one individual's speech or singing into another person's voice. Notably, certain experts, despite the legal ambiguity, have created guides on model training and cover creation, sharing links to models they've developed for others to download.

Running one of these models locally demands a certain level of technical proficiency, but a variety of browser-based alternatives have emerged to simplify the process. Products like Musicfy, Voicify, Covers, and Kits are among the newcomers aiming to streamline AI cover creation. Most of these tools require users to upload a clip of themselves or another person singing, although it's foreseeable that text-to-song capabilities are on the horizon (products like Uberduck are already implementing this for rap music).

Royalty-Free Music. Regarding royalty-free tracks, often referred to as "AI Muzak," the transition to prosumer tools has been notable. If you've ever ventured into producing content for platforms like YouTube, podcasts, or business videos, you've likely encountered the challenge of sourcing royalty-free music. While stock music libraries are available, they often present a navigational labyrinth, and the most appealing tracks tend to be overused. This has given rise to a somewhat derided musical category known for its forgettable, albeit royalty-free, quality, often labeled as "muzak" or "elevator music."

This is where AI-generated music steps in! Products like Beatoven, Soundraw, and Boomy have simplified the process of creating distinctive, royalty-free tracks, making it accessible to virtually anyone. Typically, these tools offer the option to select a genre, mood, and energy level for your composition, using these inputs to automatically generate an entirely new track. Additionally, some of these platforms enable users to fine-tune the output if it doesn't precisely align with their vision. This may involve adjusting the tempo, adding or removing specific instruments, or even reconfiguring musical notes.

Music Generation. The most thrilling prospect arising from the synergy of large-scale AI models with music is the potential it holds for bedroom producers and other non-professional musicians, even those who may not possess formal music training, to craft music of professional quality. This opens up a range of exciting capabilities, including:

- **Inpainting.** Taking a small selection of musical notes played by a producer and skillfully "filling in" the rest of the phrase.

- **Outpainting.** Enabling the extension of a given song section by predicting the subsequent bars, a feature already available in MusicGen with its "continuation" setting.

- **Audio to MIDI.** Translating audio into MIDI format, complete with pitch bend, velocity, and other MIDI attributes, utilizing tools like Spotify's Basic Pitch product where applicable.

- **Stem Separation.** Breaking down a song into its individual components, such as vocals, basslines, and percussion, often accomplished with the aid of technologies like Demucs.

You can imagine a future music producer's creative workflow as the following:

1. Select a song for sampling, ensuring all relevant rights are secured.
2. Divide the song into its constituent parts and convert an intriguing audio element into MIDI.
3. Initiate the composition process by playing a series of notes on a synthesizer and employing inpainting techniques to complete the musical phrase.
4. Extend the initial phrase by extrapolating it into several additional musical sequences using outpainting.
5. Assemble a full music track, possibly incorporating generative technology to generate unique musical elements. This might

involve replicating or expanding upon studio musicians' contributions and finalizing the track with a distinctive style.

Recently, there has been a surge in AI software products, each focusing on specific aspects of the music production process. Examples include tools for generating samples (like Soundry AI), crafting melodies (as seen with MelodyStudio), generating MIDI files (with options such as Lemonaide and AudioCipher), and even assisting with the mixing stage (exemplified by RoEx).

AI Movies

In the opening scenes of *The Frost*, a group is gathered around a fire, accompanied by barking dogs. For the viewer, this is a familiar but disconcerting setting that leaves an unsettling sense of foreboding; there's an undeniable strangeness at play in *The Frost* in part because none of the characters look quite right!

Why is that? Well, because they were made in DALL-E!

In the burgeoning scene of AI-generated filmmaking, Stephen Parker from Waymark, the Detroit-based video production company behind *The Frost*, recounts his journey: "We kind of hit a point where we just stopped fighting the desire for photographic accuracy and started leaning into the weirdness that is DALL-E" (Heaven, 2023). Parker's endeavor resulted in *The Frost*, a 12-minute movie where every shot is the creation of an image-generating AI.

Creating *The Frost* involved feeding a script written by Josh Rubin, an executive producer at Waymark who also directed the film, to OpenAI's image-generation model, DALL-E 2. After some trial and error to ensure the model's images aligned with their vision, they harnessed DALL-E 2 to produce each shot. Subsequently, they turned to D-ID, an AI tool that animates still images, giving life to these shots by making eyes blink and lips move.

"We built a world out of what DALL-E was giving us," Rubin explains. "It's a strange aesthetic, but we welcomed it with open arms. It became the look of the film" (Heaven, 2023).

Independent filmmaker Souki Mehdaoui remarks on *The Frost*'s uniqueness: "This is certainly the first generative AI film I've seen where the style feels consistent. Generating still images and puppeteering them gives it a fun collaged vibe" (Heaven, 2023).

The Frost joins a growing collection of short films produced using various generative AI tools that have emerged in recent months. While the most advanced generative video models can only produce short clips, the films produced exhibit diverse styles and techniques, from sequences resembling storyboards composed of still images, as seen in *The Frost*, to compilations of brief, second-long video clips.

In February and March of 2023, Runway, a company specializing in AI video production tools, organized an AI film festival in New York, featuring innovative works like PLSTC, Given Again, and Expanded Childhood. These creations showcased the capabilities of AI in producing otherworldly scenes, turning 2D photos into 3D virtual objects, and extending old family photos in surreal ways.

Artists and creators are often the early adopters of new technology, but the future of generative video is largely being shaped by the advertising industry. Companies like Waymark aim to incorporate generative AI into their video creation tools by offering businesses an efficient and cost-effective means to produce commercials. Such tools are already being embraced by individual content creators and small to medium-sized businesses.

While the use of generative AI in filmmaking is gaining traction, there are challenges and uncertainties. The rapid evolution of technology, copyright issues related to the use of data sets in training models, and the need for nuanced consideration make it difficult to predict the trajectory of this emerging field.

For now, filmmakers continue to experiment with these new tools. The possibilities are tantalizing, and generative AI is on the cusp of transforming the aesthetics of digital culture!

From transportation, business, finance, health, education, and now entertainment, AI is being firmly incorporated into our lives, both from a macro level to daily activities. From a job and career perspective, there are tremendous opportunities for new and emerging roles in these fields. It just takes a change in mindset to realize that we're in a time of significant job transformation.

Where Does the Future of AI Lead?

I have said it before: AI is only as good as the people who use and develop it. If we want to know what is wrong with AI, we should take a look at ourselves! Our moral compass, our intent, and our understanding of the ethical implications of AI are central to shaping its future.

As AI continues to evolve, so does our responsibility to ensure it adheres to the highest ethical standards. As a global community, we must implement safeguards that hold individuals and organizations accountable for their AI systems' consequences. Transparency, fairness, and the protection of human rights should be our guiding principles as AI revolutionaries.

Moreover, inclusivity and diversity in AI development are essential to the success of AI. By bringing together a spectrum of voices and experiences, we can mitigate biases, develop AI that serves the broader population, and tackle global challenges with greater precision.

In the changing job landscape which I talked about in Chapter 1, AI complements human skills. While AI can excel at data-driven tasks, the demand for uniquely human abilities, such as emotional intelligence and social skills, is on the rise. The jobs of the future will require complex problem-solving, creativity, empathy, and the ability to bridge the gap between AI-generated insights and practical strategies.

So, the future is not bleak—not bleak at all—lest of all for us revolutionaries! How will you, dear reader, make use of this technology in your life? Drop me a line and let me know how AI was the route to your success!

Conclusion

AI can be the route to your success in part because success looks different to different people. What do you want to accomplish in your life? Well, AI can help you accomplish it!

Think about me: a humble editor. A scholar of Marcel Proust. Now, I am a productive book publisher, with AI to assist me every step of the way! Melissa is a productive office worker who, thanks to AI, can complete her work while sipping margaritas on the beach. Bryant is using AI to trade stocks. There is something for everyone in this revolutionary technology because this revolutionary technology is a reflection of *us*. This technology is our hopes and dreams, our fears and worries—all in the form of a chatbot. The AI we interface with sounds like us because it is our creation. We ought to work with our creation rather than shun it like Frankenstein did to the monster in his Bavarian city.

The first tool our primate ancestors produced is known as the biface (The Metropolitan Museum of Art, n.d.). Also called a "hand axe," this tool was forged when a stone was sharpened to produce a cutting tool that was also decorative. That is, our ancestors wore these tools around their necks to signify their placement in a social hierarchy. The hand axe has been hypothesized to be the origin of incorrect or made up thoughts among our ancestors, because, with this tool, primates were able to hunt and bring down game, and they could conceive of situations where they were unable to hunt and bring down game because they didn't have a hand axe (Pain, 2022)! Human beings evolved because of some primate's decision to do one thing—craft a hand axe—rather than another: not craft one. We are not hairy—most of us!—because we evolved to live under roofs and wear clothes.

So, is AI any different than a biface, a roof, or a shawl? Maybe—maybe not! But, if there was a primate who was unhappy about his troupe's crafting of a hand axe, perhaps he sounded like those of us today who fear-monger about AI! In my opinion, the will to live continues in humans, and computers will probably not change that.

The calculation we as humans make every day is what helps us thrive and survive. A computer calculates because we tell it to—even AI, for now, follows our command.

The mantra of *The AI Success Route* is that, if AI helps us thrive and survive, then let us use it! If AI is indeed the route to our success, then let us not take another road—no matter how well-traveled it is. In this book, I have shown you a number of places where AI can help you with your life. I have shown you how AI has helped me take my career to the next level. AI can optimize things for you in terms of your studies, career, social life, and everything else.

Whether you take the AI success route yourself is up to you. That is out of my hands, and the beauty of being human is that you have a choice! I could only give you the upside and downside for taking the AI success route and let you make your own decision. AI revolutionaries are an open-minded few: but, we are few indeed.

I believe that, eventually, society will have to catch up with the AI revolution. By reading this book, you have shown that you are well ahead of the curve. In twenty years, it is impossible to know what would be the route to our success! But, for now, that route is AI. Shall we embark on this route or wait for the next revolution?

Resources

Other AI Tools

This section of the book continues from the AI tools discussed in Chapter 2. While these are often powered by ChatGPT and DALL-E models, there are yet other AI tools that can help you make money, get better grades, and improve your personal life. I have compiled an exhaustive list based on the domain the AI tool is used for. Keep in mind what you want to use AI for, and see if any programs on this list will fit your purposes:

Chatbots and Conversational AI

Conversational interfaces and chatbots have revolutionized the way we engage with technology and online platforms. These tools are designed to facilitate seamless interactions, whether it is through text, voice, or both. Below, I explore a selection of advanced tools that empower individuals and businesses to create, deploy, and optimize chatbots and conversational user interfaces (Khan, 2023). They may not apply or be of interest to everyone but I tried to make the list as vast and comprehensive as I could. Take a scan through.

- **API.ai (Dialogflow).** This comprehensive platform equips developers with the advanced tools they need to construct conversational user interfaces. It simplifies the creation of chatbots and voice-powered applications.

- **Chatfuel.** Creating a Facebook chatbot becomes a breeze with Chatfuel. You can design and deploy chatbots for your Facebook page without any coding knowledge.

- **Comm.ai.** Comm.ai offers the capability to integrate voice and chat APIs into websites and applications. It enhances user engagement and interaction.

- **Conversica.** A valuable tool for sales teams, Conversica deploys conversational interfaces to boost sales by engaging and nurturing leads.

- **EDDI.** This versatile platform enables users to create, test, and deploy chatbots. EDDI streamlines the chatbot development process.

- **FPT AI Platform.** With FPT AI Platform, businesses can automate interactions with end-users. This tool enhances customer support and user engagement.

- **Golem.ai.** Developers benefit from Golem.ai's natural language interpretation tool. It simplifies the integration of natural language understanding into applications.

- **Gong.** Sales professionals can leverage Gong to analyze and enhance their sales conversations and discovery calls. It offers insights for improving communication.

- **Kasisto.** Specifically tailored for the finance industry, Kasisto provides a conversational AI platform. It enhances customer experiences by enabling personalized banking interactions.

- **KITT.AI.** Creating conversational agents is made user-friendly with KITT.AI's visual interface. It simplifies the process of chatbot development.

- **Maluuba.** Maluuba focuses on teaching machines to think, reason, and communicate. It has applications in natural language understanding and reasoning.

- **Massively.** Businesses can utilize Massively to construct chatbots for various purposes, from customer service to marketing and beyond.

- **Meya.** Meya streamlines chatbot creation, training, and hosting, offering an all-in-one platform for developers.

- **MindMeld.** Often regarded as an improved version of Siri, MindMeld enhances voice and language understanding, making it a valuable addition to various applications.

- **Motion AI.** Building chatbots becomes a straightforward process with Motion AI. It offers user-friendly tools to create chatbots.

- **msg.ai.** msg.ai provides a chatbot with a management dashboard. It simplifies chatbot management and integration.

- **Octane AI.** This platform specializes in marketing automation for messaging. It helps businesses enhance customer interactions and lead generation.

- **OpenAI Gym.** Designed for reinforcement learning tasks, OpenAI Gym serves as an open-source interface. This is a valuable resource for researchers and developers in AI.

- **Orbit.** Orbit is a tool designed to help automate conversational AI. It streamlines the process of integrating chatbots into various applications.

- **Pool.** Pool acts as a personal assistant, aiding users in boosting productivity and completing tasks efficiently.

- **Recast.** A collaborative platform, Recast simplifies the creation, training, and deployment of intelligent bots, making it an ideal tool for developers and businesses.

- **Reply.ai.** Reply.ai offers a platform to build and manage conversational strategies. It streamlines chatbot development and deployment.

- **Semantic Machines.** Semantic Machines specializes in conversational AI, enhancing user experiences in work, travel, shopping, and entertainment.

- **Snips.** Snips enables users to add a voice assistant to connected products, enhancing Internet of Things (IoT) devices with voice capabilities.

- **Servo.** Servo provides a full spectrum of bot and voice interfaces, which can seamlessly integrate with existing systems.

- **UNU.ai.** UNU.ai utilizes swarm intelligence, harnessing group brainpower for chatbots. It enhances the collective knowledge and capabilities of bots.

- **Unify.** Tailored for e-commerce, Unify provides an e-commerce chatbot that improves customer experiences and boosts sales.

- **uTu.** uTu offers multi-channel bot analytics and data management, assisting businesses in understanding and optimizing chatbot performance.

- **Wechaty.** Wechaty serves as a Bot Framework for Wechat Personal Accounts. It simplifies the process of creating a bot on the WeChat platform.

- **Wit.ai.** Wit.ai empowers users to easily create text or voice-based bots for their preferred platforms, streamlining the chatbot development process.

- **Wysh.** Wysh is an enterprise-scale chatbot with integrated payment methods. It enhances the interaction between businesses and customers.

- **Zero AI.** Zero AI is a voice interface that excels in understanding meaning, intent, and context, making it a valuable tool for improving user interactions and support.

These tools represent a diverse range of applications for chatbots and conversational interfaces catering to developers, businesses, and individuals seeking enhanced user engagement, customer support, and automation across various sectors. By harnessing these advanced tools, you can unlock the potential for improved communication and streamlined operations.

Data Science
Transforming Insights with Advanced Tools

In the field of data science, a myriad of cutting-edge tools and platforms are available to transform data into actionable insights. These versatile resources cater to a wide range of data-related needs, from predictive analysis to deploying machine learning models. Below, I delve into some of these valuable tools that empower data scientists, researchers, and businesses to unlock the full potential of their data (Khan, 2023).

- **BigML:** BigML is an all-encompassing platform, offering a one-stop solution for all predictive use cases. It streamlines the process of developing machine learning models.

- **CrowdFlower.** CrowdFlower specializes in tasks like sentiment analysis and search relevance. It assists in harnessing the power of human intelligence to enhance data-driven decision-making.

- **Dataiku.** As a comprehensive data science platform, Dataiku supports the end-to-end data science lifecycle. Users can prototype, deploy, and scale data-driven projects effectively.

- **DataScience.** This enterprise-grade data science platform is tailored for both research and development (R&D) and production environments. It streamlines the collaboration and deployment of data science projects.

- **Domino Data Lab.** Domino Data Lab provides a collaborative platform that simplifies the process of building and deploying data science models. This is an ideal choice for teams looking to enhance productivity.

- **Kaggle.** Kaggle is more than just a platform; it is a vibrant community where individuals can learn, work, and engage in data science competitions. It offers an opportunity to play with and fine-tune machine learning models.

- **Katonic.ai.** Katonic.ai introduces the MLOps platform, automating the cycle of Intelligence. It aids in the management and deployment of machine learning models at scale.

- **RapidMiner.** RapidMiner is designed to boost the productivity of data science teams. It simplifies the process of data preparation and model building, making teams more efficient.

- **Seldon.** For data science teams seeking to put machine learning models into production, Seldon provides a dedicated solution. It enhances the deployment and management of models in real-world applications.

- **SherlockML.** SherlockML serves as an advanced platform for data scientists to build, test, and deploy AI algorithms. It streamlines the research and development of data-driven solutions.

- **Spark.** Spark is a powerful research engine capable of uncovering complex data patterns. It is indispensable for researchers and analysts looking to unearth valuable insights from vast datasets.

- **Tamr.** Tamr specializes in making data unification across disparate data silos achievable. It plays a pivotal role in simplifying the integration of varied data sources for analysis.

- **Trifacta.** Trifacta is a key player in the data science field, simplifying the process of structuring data for analysis. It assists in converting raw data into meaningful structures.

- **Yhat.** Data scientists benefit from Yhat's platform, which enables the swift deployment and updating of predictive models. It streamlines the transition from model development to production.

- **Yseop.** Yseop automates the generation of various types of content, from reports and websites to emails and articles. It is a valuable resource for businesses seeking to streamline content creation.

These data science tools represent a diverse ecosystem that caters to data professionals and businesses in their journey to derive actionable insights from data. From building predictive models to deploying AI algorithms, these resources play a pivotal role in enhancing efficiency, collaboration, and productivity in the data science domain.

Business Development
Powering Progress with Innovative Tools

In business development, an array of innovative tools and platforms have emerged to propel progress, enhance business operations, and foster creativity. These tools cater to a wide spectrum of needs, from predictive modeling to project management and AI development. Below, I describe some of these pioneering tools that empower developers, businesses, and teams to excel in their respective domains.

- **AnOdot.** AnOdot stands out in its ability to detect critical business incidents, offering invaluable insights to businesses and helping them stay ahead of potential issues.

- **Bonsai.** Bonsai is at the forefront of AI model development, focusing on creating adaptive, reliable, and programmable AI models that align with business needs.

- **Deckard.ai.** Project management is made more efficient with Deckard.ai. It assists in predicting project timelines, offering valuable guidance to project teams.

- **Fuzzy.ai.** Fuzzy.ai brings intelligent decision-making capabilities to web and mobile applications. It enhances user experiences by making applications smarter.

- **IBM Watson.** IBM Watson is a renowned AI platform for businesses. It encompasses a wide range of AI-powered solutions designed to address diverse business challenges.

- **Gigster.** Gigster simplifies the process of finding the right teams for projects. It connects businesses with talented professionals, streamlining project development.

- **Kite.** Kite augments coding environments with web-accessible knowledge, making it easier for developers to access relevant information while coding.

- **Layer 6 AI.** Layer 6 AI introduces a deep learning platform that excels in prediction and personalization. It enables businesses to leverage AI for tailored solutions.

- **Morph:** Developing chatbots for business becomes a breeze with Morph. It offers user-friendly tools for creating intelligent chatbots.

- **Neural Network Libraries by Sony.** Sony demonstrates its commitment to deep learning by releasing its own open-source deep learning framework, making it accessible to the development community.

- **Ozz.** Ozz elevates the capabilities of AI bots by facilitating self-learning. It is an invaluable resource for improving bot intelligence.

- **RainforestQA.** Rapid web and mobile app testing is a reality with RainforestQA. It expedites the testing process, ensuring the quality of applications.

- **SignifAI.** SignifAI plays a crucial role in enhancing server uptime and predicting downtime. This is indispensable for businesses reliant on uninterrupted services.

- **Turtle.** Turtle is a multifaceted platform, offering project management and chat software that is user-friendly and ideal for team collaboration.

- **TensorFlow Neural Network Playground.** The TensorFlow neural network playground provides an interactive environment for users to experiment with neural networks visually, fostering a better understanding of their capabilities and functions.

These business development tools represent a dynamic landscape that supports businesses, project teams, and developers in their journey to innovate and create. From predictive modeling to AI enhancement, these resources are instrumental in driving progress and excellence in business development.

Vehicles
Pioneering Solutions for Smarter and Autonomous Transportation

In the realm of vehicle technology, several groundbreaking tools and platforms have emerged to usher in a new era of transportation. These tools are designed to enhance the functionality and intelligence of vehicles, leading to smarter cars and paving the way for autonomous driving (Khan, 2023). Below, I explore two notable tools that are at the forefront of revolutionizing the vehicle industry:

- **Vinli.** Vinli is a transformative solution that has the power to turn any conventional car into a smart, connected vehicle. By integrating Vinli's technology, vehicles gain the ability to access a range of intelligent features and connectivity, effectively transforming them into vehicles of the future. This tool offers drivers an array of advanced capabilities, such as real-time vehicle data, diagnostics, and a connection to the broader world of IoT (Internet of Things).

- **Apollo (by Baidu):** Baidu, a technology giant, has introduced Apollo, an innovative open-source platform that is dedicated to the development of autonomous vehicles. With the aim of accelerating the realization of self-driving cars, Apollo provides a wealth of resources, including software, hardware, and knowledge, to developers and automotive manufacturers. This robust platform is engineered to address the complexities of autonomous vehicle development, such as perception, planning, and control. By making Apollo accessible, Baidu is empowering the broader automotive community to collectively pioneer the future of transportation.

These vehicle-related tools exemplify a paradigm shift in the automotive industry, propelling the evolution of vehicles towards a future characterized by intelligent connectivity and autonomous driving. While Vinli focuses on making existing cars smarter and more connected, Apollo serves as a catalyst for the development of self-driving vehicles—fostering collaboration and innovation in the pursuit of a safer and more efficient mode of transportation.

Insurance and Legal
Cutting-Edge Solutions for Legal Guidance and Safe Driving Incentives

Innovative tools have emerged to address legal issues and promote safer driving practices. These tools leverage technology to provide valuable assistance and encourage responsible behavior. Below, I describe two noteworthy tools that are redefining the landscape of insurance and legal support:

- **Docubot.** Docubot is a revolutionary tool designed to offer expert guidance and advice on legal matters. This sophisticated platform serves as a virtual legal advisor, providing insights and recommendations to individuals seeking assistance with legal issues. Whether your issue has to do with contract review, legal documentation, or general legal inquiries, Docubot employs advanced algorithms and a wealth of legal knowledge to provide accurate and timely advice.

- **Driveway.** Driveway introduces an innovative approach to enhancing road safety by tracking and rewarding responsible drivers. This tool employs telematics and data analytics to monitor driving habits and identify safe driving practices. It encourages drivers to adopt and maintain safer behaviors behind the wheel through a rewards-based system. By promoting safe driving practices, Driveway not only benefits individual drivers but also contributes to the overall improvement of road safety.

These tools in the insurance and legal sectors exemplify a fusion of cutting-edge technology and essential services. Docubot offers legal guidance in an accessible and efficient manner, while Driveway harnesses data to incentivize safer driving practices.

Personal Tools
Elevating Everyday Life with AI Assistants and Smart Solutions

It goes without saying that AI can help us improve our personal life in addition to making money and getting better grades! A vibrant ecosystem of innovative technologies and virtual assistants has emerged to enhance the daily lives of individuals across various spheres. These intelligent tools cater to a multitude of needs, from streamlining tasks to providing companionship. Below, I explore a selection of cutting-edge personal tools that redefine convenience, efficiency, and the way we interact with technology (Khan, 2023):

- **AIHelperBot:** AIHelperBot simplifies the creation of SQL queries using AI, streamlining data analysis and reporting.

- **Amazon Echo / Alexa:** This iconic duo represents an everyday personal assistant for in-home settings. With voice commands, they assist in various tasks, from setting reminders to controlling smart home devices.

- **Apple Siri:** Siri is the ever-present personal assistant available on Apple's iPhone and Mac devices, providing quick access to information and performing tasks via voice commands.

- **Brin.** Brin is designed to empower individuals with data-driven insights, helping them make more informed and intelligent business decisions.

- **Chatfuel.** For those looking to harness the power of chatbots, Chatfuel enables the rapid creation of Facebook chatbots, streamlining customer interactions and automating responses.

- **Findo.** Findo serves as a smart search assistant, helping users efficiently locate information across emails, files, and personal cloud storage.

- **Fembot:** This AI creation offers companionship as a virtual girlfriend, reflecting the evolving realm of AI in personal relationships.

- **Fin.** As a robust personal assistant, Fin aids users in various daily tasks, making life more organized and efficient.

- **Focus.** Focus supports users in enhancing productivity, providing assistance in task prioritization and time management.

- **Gatebox.** This innovative creation brings a holographic anime assistant to life within an espresso machine, showcasing the imaginative possibilities of personal AI.

- **Google Assistant.** Google Assistant is an omnipresent personal aide, delivering assistance across a myriad of daily needs and questions.

- **Howdy.** Howdy offers a friendly, trainable bot designed to assist Slack teams with their work-related activities, fostering collaboration and efficiency.

- **Hound.** Much like other everyday personal assistants, Hound is built to answer questions and perform tasks through voice commands.

- **Julie Desk.** Targeted at C-Suite professionals, Julie Desk is a meeting scheduling assistant, streamlining the process of organizing and managing appointments.

- **Kono.** Kono operates as a meeting scheduling assistant, simplifying the coordination of meetings and appointments.

- **Lifos.** These dynamic independent entities interact with the web and social platforms, offering personalized assistance for online activities.

- **Ling.** Ling, akin to Amazon Echo, delivers voice-activated support in various daily tasks, from information retrieval to controlling smart devices.

- **Luka.** Luka serves as a chatbot messenger that enables communication with both individuals and other chatbots, facilitating seamless exchanges.

- **Lyra:** With a focus on environmental consciousness, Lyra monitors and analyzes carbon emissions, contributing to eco-awareness.

- **Magic.** Magic introduces a hassle-free service where users can text a special phone number to request virtually anything they need, showcasing the power of AI-assisted convenience.
- **Microsoft Cortana.** Similar to Siri, Cortana is a voice-controlled virtual assistant on Microsoft Windows, providing personalized recommendations and search capabilities.
- **Mimetic.** This tool is ideal for meeting scheduling, streamlining the coordination of appointments and commitments.
- **My Ally.** My Ally focuses on meeting scheduling and calendar management, reducing the administrative burden of organizing appointments.
- **Mycroft.** As the world's first open-source voice assistant, Mycroft empowers users to customize and control their digital interactions.
- **myWave.** This chatbot offers comprehensive support throughout daily life, showcasing the versatility of AI-driven companions.

- **Remi.** Remi resembles Siri in function, providing assistance with an intuitive interface.

- **Replika.** Replika stands out as an AI friend that evolves and learns through text conversations, making it a unique and evolving companion.

- **SkipFlag.** With automated organization and discovery, SkipFlag streamlines work processes, leading to more efficient collaboration.

- **Spoken.** This virtual assistant combines the power of AI with a user-friendly interface to address various tasks and requests.

- **Vesper.** Tailored for C-Suite professionals, Vesper serves as a virtual assistant, offering support for daily operations and business tasks.

- **Viv.** Viv represents a step forward in personal AI, with capabilities that surpass those of Siri, providing advanced assistance.

- **x.ai.** x.ai assists users in automating meeting scheduling, simplifying the process of organizing and coordinating appointments.

- **Zoom.ai.** As a personal assistant designed for the workplace, Zoom.ai enhances productivity and efficiency, providing support for work-related tasks and queries.

These personal tools exemplify the incredible potential of AI to enhance everyday life, streamline tasks, and redefine our relationships with technology. They cater to a diverse array of needs, highlighting the boundless possibilities for AI-driven convenience and assistance in our daily routines.

Writing Tools
Revolutionizing Content Creation with AI-Powered Assistance

In the world of content creation and written communication, the integration of AI has brought forth a range of innovative tools designed to assist individuals and teams in generating compelling, SEO-friendly content. These AI-powered writing tools cater to a diverse set of needs, from marketing and SEO to collaborative editing and content ideation. Let us explore some of these game-changing writing tools that have transformed the way we create written materials (Khan, 2023):

- **Jasperi AI.** Positioned as an AI writer for marketing and content teams, Jasperi AI simplifies the content creation process by generating marketing materials, website content, and more. With AI-driven insights, it enhances the quality and effectiveness of written communication.

- **Writesonic.** Writesonic steps into the realm of AI-powered content generation, specializing in crafting SEO-friendly content. It efficiently generates website copy, blog posts, and marketing materials, ensuring that content aligns with the latest SEO best practices.

- **Taskade AI.** Taskade AI offers a multi-faceted approach to content creation, focusing on AI outlining and mind mapping with collaborative editing. This tool empowers teams to brainstorm, outline, and co-create written content with ease, fostering a creative and efficient environment for idea generation and content development.

These writing tools exemplify how AI has transformed content creation by enabling individuals and teams to produce high-quality, SEO-optimized written materials, collaborate seamlessly, and streamline the content ideation process. They embody the future of written communication, where AI-driven assistance elevates the efficiency and quality of content production.

Health/Medical Tools
Transforming Healthcare with AI-Powered Support

In the landscape of healthcare and well-being, the integration of AI has ushered in a new era of innovative tools dedicated to promoting healthier lives and providing support for various medical needs. These AI-driven health and medical tools cover a wide spectrum, offering solutions for personal health management, mental health support, and assistance with specific medical conditions. I will delve into these remarkable tools that are reshaping the healthcare industry (Khan, 2023):

- **Abi.** As your virtual health assistant, Abi is designed to provide users with comprehensive health-related information and guidance, empowering them to make informed decisions about their well-being.

- **Ada.** Ada lends a helping hand when you're feeling unwell. This AI-powered tool assists users in assessing their symptoms and provides recommendations for appropriate next steps, ensuring personalized healthcare guidance.

- **Airi.** Serving as a personal health coach, Airi motivates and guides individuals on their journey towards better health and well-being.

It offers support and encouragement to help users achieve their health goals.

- **Alz.ai.** Alz.ai is a valuable resource for those caring for loved ones with Alzheimer's disease. This tool offers support and information to aid in the compassionate and informed care of individuals with Alzheimer's.

- **Bitesnap.** Bitesnap leverages AI to recognize and track food items through meal photos, assisting users in monitoring their calorie intake and fostering healthier dietary choices.

- **doc.ai.** Streamlining the understanding of lab results, doc.ai makes complex medical data more accessible. It translates lab results into easy-to-grasp insights, ensuring that users can better comprehend their health information.

- **Gyan.** Gyan serves as a reliable health companion, helping users navigate from symptoms to potential conditions. It offers insights into likely health conditions based on user-provided symptoms, enhancing health awareness.

- **Joy.** Joy is a dedicated platform for tracking and improving mental health. It empowers users to monitor their mental well-being and access resources to enhance their emotional health.

- **Kiwi.** Kiwi is a trusted ally for those looking to reduce or quit smoking. It provides guidance and support to individuals on their journey to a smoke-free life.

- **Tess by X2AI.** With Tess, a therapist is in your pocket. Tess is an AI-driven therapeutic tool that offers mental health support, providing a convenient and accessible platform for emotional well-being.

- **Sleep.ai.** Sleep.ai specializes in diagnosing snoring and tooth grinding, shedding light on potential sleep-related issues and facilitating informed decisions about sleep quality.

These health and medical tools underscore the significant impact of AI in healthcare. They empower individuals to take charge of their health, seek support for mental well-being, and access resources for managing specific medical conditions. These AI-driven tools epitomize the transformative potential of technology in the healthcare industry.

Travel AI Tools
Navigating Your Journeys with AI-Powered Assistance

In travel and exploration, AI has emerged as an invaluable companion by enriching our experiences and simplifying the complex landscape of journey planning. AI-powered travel tools cover an array of functions, offering support for seamless navigation, scheduling, and even safety enhancement during your adventures. Let us discuss these remarkable AI-driven travel tools that have redefined the way we embark on our journeys (Khan, 2023):

- **Ada.** A trusty chatbot, Ada is designed to assist travelers in navigating unfamiliar territories and making well-informed decisions. Whether this involves providing destination information or offering travel recommendations, Ada is your travel buddy.

- **Emma.** Emma takes the hassle out of meeting travel planning by automatically calculating and incorporating travel time into your itinerary, ensuring you stay punctual and organized.

- **ETA.** With ETA, managing travel itineraries and meetings becomes a breeze. This tool streamlines travel logistics, making it simpler to keep track of schedules and locations.

- **HelloGbye.** Planning complex trips is a cinch with HelloGbye. This AI-powered platform lets you book multifaceted journeys using simple voice commands, reducing the stress of intricate trip planning.

- **Mezi.** Mezi steps in to streamline various aspects of travel, from booking flights and hotels to securing restaurant reservations. This all-in-one tool ensures that your travel arrangements are smooth and hassle-free.

- **Nexar.** Nexar introduces safety to your travel adventures with its dash cam app. By recording your journeys, it promotes safer driving practices, enhancing road safety for all.

- **Ready.** Ready is your go-to source for traffic forecasting and travel time prediction. Planning your routes and scheduling your travels becomes more efficient with real-time traffic insights.

- **Spatial.** Offering a unique perspective on cities, Spatial unveils the social layer of urban destinations. It enriches your travel experiences by providing insights into local cultures, traditions, and events.

These AI travel tools have revolutionized the way we navigate the world. They ensure that our journeys are enriched with support, safety, and efficiency, guaranteeing a smoother travel experience. The presence of AI in the realm of travel has ushered in a new era of convenience and accessibility, facilitating seamless exploration and adventure.

Finance AI Tools

Your Financial Guardians and Investment Advisors

In the domain of personal and business finance, AI has emerged as a powerful tool to enhance our financial well-being and reshape how we manage our money. AI-powered finance tools encompass a wide spectrum of functions, from offering swift financial insights to providing personalized investment advice. Let us discuss these remarkable AI-driven financial tools that have revolutionized the way we navigate the financial landscape (Khan, 2023):

- **Abe.** If you seek fast answers about your finances, Abe is your go-to AI companion. Abe provides quick and reliable financial information, making financial decision-making a breeze.

- **Andy.** Andy steps in as a personal tax accountant, simplifying the intricacies of tax management. With Andy's assistance, navigating tax-related matters becomes a less daunting task.

- **Ara.** Keeping a tight budget is crucial for financial stability, and Ara is designed to assist with just that. This AI tool helps you manage your expenses and stay on top of your financial goals.

- **Bond.** Achieving your financial aspirations is made easier with Bond. This tool is your financial ally, offering insights and strategies to help you reach your financial objectives.

- **Mylo.** Mylo's ingenious approach involves rounding up your everyday purchases and investing the spare change. By doing so, it contributes to your financial growth and investment portfolio.

- **Olivia.** Olivia is a comprehensive financial manager. From tracking your expenses to offering investment advice, it helps you maintain control over your financial landscape.

- **Responsive.** When it comes to active portfolio management, Responsive offers institutional-grade expertise. It optimizes your investment portfolio, ensuring your financial assets are in the best hands.

- **Roger.** Simplify bill payments with the help of Roger. This AI tool streamlines the bill-paying process, ensuring your financial obligations are met without complications.

- **Xoe.ai.** Xoe.ai serves as your AI lending chatbot. It provides valuable insights and guidance for individuals and businesses looking to explore lending options.

These AI finance tools have redefined the way we manage our finances. They ensure our financial journey is marked by convenience, reliability, and the potential for growth. AI's presence in the world of finance has not only enhanced our decision-making but has also facilitated more informed investments and smarter financial management. With these tools by your side, you can navigate the financial landscape with confidence and efficiency.

Language / Translation AI Tools
Bridging Communication Gaps and Cultural Divides

In an increasingly interconnected world, communication knows no bounds. Language and translation AI tools have stepped in to break down linguistic barriers and facilitate the exchange of information, knowledge, and culture across the globe. These advanced AI tools, underpinned by powerful neural networks, enable seamless language translation and transcend traditional language constraints. I will outline these remarkable AI-driven language and translation tools that are reshaping the way we communicate (Khan, 2023):

- **Microsoft Translator.** Powered by neural networks, Microsoft Translator stands as a versatile language translator. It offers swift and accurate translations across a wide range of languages, enhancing communication in both personal and professional spheres. From conversations to written documents, this tool has proven indispensable.

- **Watson.ai.** Watson.ai takes on the challenging realms of legal, academic, and financial translations. As an AI tool, it excels in providing precise and context-aware translations in domains where accuracy is paramount. Legal documents, academic papers, and financial records are all translated with a commitment to precision.

These language and translation AI tools are instrumental in bridging communication gaps and ensuring that information flows effortlessly across linguistic and cultural divides. Whether you're a global business seeking to expand your reach or an individual connecting with people from different corners of the world, these AI-driven tools empower you with the ability to communicate with ease and accuracy. The future of communication is bright, thanks to these language and translation AI innovations.

IoT/IioT
Transforming Everyday Life and Industry Through Smart Connectivity

The Internet of Things (IoT) and Industrial Internet of Things (IIoT) are revolutionizing the way we interact with our surroundings, whether in the comfort of our homes or in the complex landscape of industrial operations. These technological innovations are fueling smart connectivity, providing us with more control, convenience, and efficiency than ever before. Let us explore some notable IoT and IIoT solutions that are reshaping the world (Khan, 2023):

- **Aerial.** A home activity, movement, and identity sensor, Aerial is instrumental in making your living space smarter. It helps you monitor and control various aspects of your home environment, from security to energy efficiency.

- **Bridge.ai.** Focused on speech and sound, Bridge.ai is a smart-home platform that enhances the way you interact with your home. By harnessing the power of voice and sound, it provides a new level of convenience and automation to your daily life.

- **Cubic.** Serving as a central hub for your smart home devices, Cubic simplifies the management of your connected technologies. It brings together disparate devices into a unified ecosystem, making smart living more accessible and coherent.

- **Grojo.** In the world of smart agriculture and horticulture, Grojo shines as a grow room controller and monitoring system. It optimizes the conditions for plant growth, ensuring that crops flourish with precision.

- **Home.** With a focus on autonomous home operations through connected devices, Home elevates the way we interact with our living spaces. It empowers homeowners with advanced control and automation capabilities, from lighting to security.

- **Hello.** Sleep is a vital part of our lives, and Hello offers a solution to monitor and enhance it. Through data-driven insights, it helps individuals achieve better sleep patterns and overall well-being.

- **Josh.** Providing whole-house voice control, Josh streamlines the management of smart devices in your home. Whether this is in terms of lighting, climate, or entertainment, Josh ensures that your voice commands are heard and executed.

- **Mycroft.** As the world's first open-source voice assistant, Mycroft puts the power of voice control and automation in the hands of developers and enthusiasts. It offers endless possibilities for voice-based applications and services.

- **Nanit.** For parents, Nanit is a game-changer. This is a baby monitor that not only keeps an eye on the baby but also measures sleep patterns and caregiver interactions, providing invaluable insights.

- **Nest.** Renowned for its range of in-home devices, Nest has set the standard for smart living. From thermostats to security and alarms, Nest products offer a comprehensive solution for modern homes.

These IoT and IIoT solutions exemplify the remarkable transformation that smart connectivity brings to our everyday lives and industries. They enhance our control, security, and efficiency, ensuring that we live and work in environments that are safer, more convenient, and more interconnected than ever before.

Research Tools
Revolutionizing Information Analysis and Retrieval

In the space of information and data, research tools play a crucial role in helping us make sense of vast amounts of content, conduct thorough investigations, and extract valuable insights. These innovative solutions have redefined the way we approach research and analysis. I will describe some noteworthy research tools that are changing the game (Khan, 2023):

- **Apollo.** Research often involves sifting through lengthy articles and PDF documents.

Apollo simplifies this process by breaking down complex content into quick, readable dot points. It offers a time-efficient way to grasp key information from extensive materials.

- **Ferret.ai.** When you're deep in the research process, Ferret.ai becomes an invaluable companion. It aids researchers by summarizing articles and enhancing search capabilities. This tool streamlines the path to discovery by providing concise, accessible information.

- **Iris.** Research papers can be dense and challenging to interpret. Iris steps in to make the journey smoother. It assists researchers in visualizing concepts within research papers, making it easier to understand and navigate complex academic literature.

These research tools reflect the ongoing innovation in information analysis and retrieval. They cater to a wide range of needs, from simplifying content consumption to enhancing search capabilities and providing visual aids for complex research. As a result, researchers have at their disposal a suite of resources that empower them to uncover knowledge and insights more efficiently than ever before.

Empowering Writers
AI Writing Assistants

In the digital age, writing has transcended pen and paper to become an integral part of online communication, marketing, and content creation. AI-powered writing assistants are making a significant impact by helping writers of all kinds craft high-quality content, streamline their work, and enhance productivity. Here are some noteworthy AI writing assistants (Khan, 2023):

- **Jasper.** Jasper is your creative companion for fast content creation. With artificial intelligence at its core, Jasper accelerates the writing process, making it easier to generate content efficiently.

- **Compose AI.** Compose AI, available as a Chrome extension, supercharges your writing productivity. It offers AI-powered autocompletion, cutting down your writing time by a remarkable 40%.

- **Rytr.** Rytr is your go-to AI writing assistant for producing high-quality content. It aids in creating engaging and polished written material, saving you time and effort.

- **Wordtune.** Wordtune serves as a personal writing assistant, helping you refine your writing for clarity and impact. This is a valuable tool for enhancing the quality of your content.

- **HyperWrite.** With HyperWrite, you can write confidently and efficiently, from conceptualization to the final draft. It streamlines your writing journey and boosts productivity.

- **Moonbeam.** Moonbeam accelerates the process of creating compelling blogs. This is your shortcut to producing top-notch content in a fraction of the time.

- **Copy.ai.** If you're in the realm of marketing, Copy.ai is your ally for crafting persuasive marketing copy and engaging content through AI-powered assistance.

- **Anyword.** Anyword's AI writing assistant excels at generating effective copy for various applications. It simplifies the task of producing compelling content.

- **Contenda.** Contenda empowers you to create content that resonates with your audience by leveraging existing content as a foundation.

- **Hypotenuse AI.** Transform a handful of keywords into original and insightful articles, product descriptions, and social media copy with Hypotenuse AI.

- **Lavender.** Lavender serves as an email assistant, enhancing your email communication efficiency and increasing your response rate.

- **Lex.** Lex is a word processor infused with artificial intelligence, enabling faster and more efficient writing.

- **Jenni.** Jenni acts as the ultimate writing assistant, saving you hours in thinking and writing time, whether you're a professional writer or a content creator.

- **LAIKA.** LAIKA is your personalized creative partner, trained on your writing style to assist you in content creation.

- **QuillBot.** QuillBot is an AI-powered paraphrasing tool, ensuring your writing is precise and engaging.

- **Postwise.** For social media management, Postwise aids in crafting tweets, scheduling posts, and growing your following using AI insights.

- **Copysmith.** Copysmith caters to enterprise and e-commerce content creation, offering an AI-based solution for generating compelling and relevant content.

These AI writing assistants have significantly changed the writing landscape, making it more accessible, efficient, and impactful. From content creation to marketing copy and email assistance, these tools empower writers to enhance their writing, boost productivity, and achieve their goals more effectively.

Enhancing ChatGPT
Extensions for a More Productive Experience

As the capabilities of AI models like ChatGPT continue to evolve, a multitude of extensions have emerged to augment the functionality and utility of these models. These extensions are designed to enhance the user experience, making it more versatile, productive, and engaging. Here are some notable ChatGPT extensions:

- **WebChatGPT.** WebChatGPT integrates web search results with ChatGPT prompts, providing users with relevant information from the internet and enhancing the scope of responses.

- **GPT for Sheets and Docs.** This extension brings ChatGPT's conversational power to Google Sheets and Google Docs, allowing users to generate content, brainstorm ideas, and collaborate more effectively.

- **YouTube Summary with ChatGPT.** ChatGPT can now assist in summarizing YouTube videos, simplifying the process of extracting key insights and information.

- **ChatGPT Prompt Genius.** Discover, share, and import the most effective prompts for ChatGPT. This extension enables users to save chat histories locally and easily access and reuse them.

- **ChatGPT for Search Engines.** Users can view ChatGPT responses alongside search results from popular engines like Google, Bing, and DuckDuckGo, streamlining the process of finding information online.

- **ShareGPT.** Share your ChatGPT conversations with others and explore conversations shared by the community, creating an environment for collective learning and collaboration.

- **Merlin.** Merlin is a ChatGPT Plus extension that can be used on all websites. It enhances the ChatGPT experience across various online platforms.

- **ChatGPT Writer.** Generate complete emails and messages using ChatGPT AI, simplifying communication and content creation.

- **ChatGPT for Jupyter.** This extension adds useful helper functions to Jupyter Notebooks and Jupyter Lab, powered by ChatGPT, for more efficient data analysis and content generation.

- **editGPT.** Proofread, edit, and track changes in your content within the ChatGPT interface, ensuring polished and error-free communication.

These ChatGPT extensions exemplify the power of AI and the ever-expanding possibilities they bring to diverse aspects of our digital lives. By combining AI-driven capabilities with various online platforms, they help us streamline tasks, generate content, access relevant information, and collaborate more effectively. The result is a more dynamic and versatile AI experience!

References

Analyst Answers. (2023). AI Trading: Success Rates & Profitability. Retrieved from https://analystanswers.com/ai-trading-success-rates-profitability/

Bailey, R. (2014, July 2). Healthy Body and a Sound Mind? [Blog post]. Psychology Today. Retrieved from https://www.psychologytoday.com/intl/blog/smart-moves/201407/healthy-body-and-a-sound-mind

Balderson, K. (2023, July 7). 27 AI In Education Statistics You Should Know. Retrieved from https://mspoweruser.com/ai-in-education-statistics/#3_43_of_US_college_students_admit_to_using_AI_tools_like_ChatGPT_for_studying

Castillo, L. (2023, October 15). Must-Know AI Replacing Jobs Statistics [Latest Data 2023]. Gitnux. Retrieved from https://blog.gitnux.com/ai-replacing-jobs-statistics/

Delta Wealth Advisors. (2023). What Is the Success Rate of a Financial Advisor? Retrieved from https://deltawealthadvisors.com/blog/what-is-the-success-rate-of-a-financial-advisor

FitnessAI. (n.d.). FitnessAI — Get Stronger, Faster with Artificial Intelligence. Retrieved November 10, 2023, from https://www.fitnessai.com/

Gettysburg College. (2023). One third of your life is spent at work. Gettysburg College. https://www.gettysburg.edu/news/stories?id=79db7b34-630c-4f49-ad32-4ab9ea48e72b

GymGenie. (n.d.). Home. Retrieved November 10, 2023, from https://gymgenie.vercel.app/

Hare, J. (2023, January 27). You can't ban the bot, educators say as they struggle with ChatGPT. The Australian Financial Review. Retrieved from https://www.afr.com/work-and-careers/education/you-can-t-ban-the-bot-educators-say-as-they-struggle-with-chatgpt-20230125-p5cfed

Heaven, W. D. (2023, June 1). Exclusive: Watch the world premiere of the AI-generated short film The Frost. MIT Technology Review. Retrieved from https://www.technologyreview.com/2023/06/01/1073858/surreal-ai-generative-video-changing-film/

Hironde, J. (2023, August 31). AI's Impact On The Future Of Consumer Behavior And Expectations. Forbes. Retrieved from https://www.forbes.com/sites/forbestechcouncil/2023/08/31/ais-impact-on-the-future-of-consumer-behavior-and-expectations/?sh=95449857f6db.

Hsu, J. (2023, January 12). Should schools ban ChatGPT or embrace the technology instead? New

Scientist. Retrieved from https://www.newscientist.com/article/2354663-should-schools-ban-chatgpt-or-embrace-the-technology-instead/

iris Dating app. Retrieved from https://www.irisdating.com/#:~:text=iris%20Dating%20applies%20artificial%20intelligence,attracted%20to%20someone%20like%20you

Johnson, A. (2023, January 18). ChatGPT In Schools: Here's Where It's Banned—And How It Could Potentially Help Students. Forbes. Retrieved from https://www.forbes.com/sites/ariannajohnson/2023/01/18/chatgpt-in-schools-heres-where-its-banned-and-how-it-could-potentially-help-students/?sh=31222916e2c6

Khan, S. (2023). The Ultimate List of AI Tools: Discover the Best Tools for Every Category. Medium. https://medium.com/@skhans/the-ultimate-list-of-ai-tools-discover-the-best-tools-for-every-category-a98288b24364

Kohn, E. (2013). How forests think: Toward an anthropology beyond the human. University of California Press.

Larson, L. (2012). It's Time to Turn the Digital Page: Preservice Teachers Explore E-Book Reading. *Journal of Adolescent and Adult Literacy* 56(4), 280-290.

Laviola, E. (2023, July 11). Types of AI in Healthcare: Explained [With Use Cases]. Retrieved from https://healthtechmagazine.net/article/2023/07/types-ai-in-healthcare-perfcon

Licholai, G. (2023, September 20). Congress Navigating The Future Of AI In Healthcare. Retrieved from https://www.forbes.com/sites/greglicholai/2023/09/20/congress-navigating-the-future-of-ai-in-health/?sh=18634bfe1f2b

McKie, R. (2018, May 6). No death and an enhanced life: Is the future transhuman? The Guardian. Retrieved from https://www.theguardian.com/technology/2018/may/06/no-death-and-an-enhanced-life-is-the-future-transhuman

Mearian, L. (n.d.). Schools look to ban ChatGPT, students use it anyway. Computerworld. Retrieved from https://www.computerworld.com/article/3694195/schools-look-to-ban-chatgpt-students-use-it-anyway.html.

The Metropolitan Museum of Art. (n.d.). Biface, commonly referred to as a hand ax | Lower Paleolithic Period | The Metropolitan Museum of Art. Retrieved from https://www.metmuseum.org/art/collection/search/573104

Mok, A., & Zinkula, J. (2023, September 4). ChatGPT: the 10 Jobs Most at Risk of Being Replaced by AI. Business Insider. Retrieved from https://www.businessinsider.com/chatgpt-jobs-at-risk-replacement-artificial-intelligence-ai-labor-trends-2023-02#customer-service-agents-10

Moore, J., & Acharya, A. (2023, November 9). The Future of Music: How Generative AI Is Transforming the Music Industry. Retrieved from https://a16z.com/the-future-of-music-how-generative-ai-is-transforming-the-music-industry/
Napolitano, E. (2023, June 2). AI eliminated nearly 4,000 jobs in May, report says. CBS News. Retrieved from https://www.cbsnews.com/news/ai-job-losses-artificial-intelligence-challenger-report/

Pain, R. (2021). Stone tools, predictive processing, and the evolution of language. *Mind & Language* 38(3), 619-642. https://doi.org/10.1111/mila.12419

Perez, S. (2020, February 6). Pew: 30% of US adults have used online dating; 12% found a committed relationship from it. TechCrunch. Retrieved from https://techcrunch.com/2020/02/06/pew-30-of-us-adults-have-used-online-dating-12-found-a-committed-relationships-from-it/?guccounter=1&guce_referrer=aHR0cHM6Ly93d3cuYmluZy5jb20v&guce_referrer_sig=AQAAAKJS0

QS5IirAhcLgT6qYvoNYhS7S6LsbGtDwdQrDHVMJ
ci5DX7XjdkQUbThTtdlgm1WVGQ2eryx1Qxot563Zr
OX6KgqVfUMZ0zKr4xV0vnZvnTOzl1fCJzxyzyx8jK
dI59UaODWV7B81ZuXyIefQZonG6zLxzD2nkFYKA
WcxD6U9

Perry, M. (2019, December 18). More evidence that it's really hard to beat the market over time: 95% of finance professionals can't do it. Retrieved from https://www.aei.org/carpe-diem/more-evidence-that-its-really-hard-to-beat-the-market-over-time-95-of-finance-professionals-cant-do-it/

Rebelo, M. (2023, August 1). The 7 best AI scheduling assistants in 2023. Zapier. Retrieved from https://zapier.com/blog/best-ai-scheduling/

Rebelo, M. (2023, August 1). The 11 best AI tools for social media management in 2023. Zapier. Retrieved from https://zapier.com/blog/best-ai-social-media-management/

Roose, K. (2023, January 12). Don't Ban ChatGPT in Schools. Teach With It. The New York Times. Retrieved from https://www.nytimes.com/2023/01/12/technology/chatgpt-schools-teachers.html

The Second Angle. (2023, February 15). 8 Best AI Investment Tools. Retrieved from https://thesecondangle.com/8-best-ai-investment-tools/#:~:text=Check%20out%20our%20list%20of

%20the%208%20best,7.%20Ellevest%20…%208%208.%20Blackbox%20Stocks%20

ThinkML Team. (2022, June 8). AI in Nutrition: Top 10 Fitness Apps and Startups. Retrieved from https://thinkml.ai/ai-in-nutrition-top-10-fitness-apps-and-startups/

Skandul, E. (2023, August 14). AI Will Radically Reshape Job Market, Global Economy, Employee Productivity. Business Insider. https://www.businessinsider.com/ai-radically-reshape-job-market-global-economy-employee-labor-innovation-2023-8

Thomson, J. (2023, April 9). 3 rules for robots from Isaac Asimov — and one he missed. Big Think. Retrieved from https://bigthink.com/the-future/3-rules-for-robots-isaac-asimov-one-rule-he-missed/

UNESCO. (2023, June 1). UNESCO survey: Less than 10% of schools and universities have formal guidance on AI. Retrieved from https://www.unesco.org/en/articles/unesco-survey-less-10-schools-and-universities-have-formal-guidance-ai

UoPeople. (n.d.). AI In Education: Where Is It Now And What Is The Future. Retrieved from https://www.uopeople.edu/blog/ai-in-education-where-is-it-now-and-what-is-the-future/

Vallance, C. (2023, March 28). AI could replace equivalent of 300 million jobs - report. BBC News. Retrieved from https://www.bbc.com/news/technology-65102150.

%20the%208%20best,7.%20Ellevest%20...%208%208.%20Blackbox%20Stocks%20

ThinkML Team. (2022, June 8). AI in Nutrition: Top 10 Fitness Apps and Startups. Retrieved from https://thinkml.ai/ai-in-nutrition-top-10-fitness-apps-and-startups/

Skandul, E. (2023, August 14). AI Will Radically Reshape Job Market, Global Economy, Employee Productivity. Business Insider. https://www.businessinsider.com/ai-radically-reshape-job-market-global-economy-employee-labor-innovation-2023-8

Thomson, J. (2023, April 9). 3 rules for robots from Isaac Asimov — and one he missed. Big Think. Retrieved from https://bigthink.com/the-future/3-rules-for-robots-isaac-asimov-one-rule-he-missed/

UNESCO. (2023, June 1). UNESCO survey: Less than 10% of schools and universities have formal guidance on AI. Retrieved from https://www.unesco.org/en/articles/unesco-survey-less-10-schools-and-universities-have-formal-guidance-ai

UoPeople. (n.d.). AI In Education: Where Is It Now And What Is The Future. Retrieved from https://www.uopeople.edu/blog/ai-in-education-where-is-it-now-and-what-is-the-future/

Vallance, C. (2023, March 28). AI could replace equivalent of 300 million jobs - report. BBC News. Retrieved from https://www.bbc.com/news/technology-65102150.

www.ingramcontent.com/pod-product-compliance
Lightning Source LLC
Chambersburg PA
CBHW070121110526
44587CB00017BA/2869